SOCIAL SECURITY LAW

Second Edition

by
Margaret C. Jasper

Oceana's Legal Almanac Series:
Law for the Layperson

2004
Oceana Publications, Inc.
Dobbs Ferry, New York

You may order this or any Oceana publication by visiting Oceana's website at http://www.oceanalaw.com

Library of Congress Control Number: 2004105894

ISBN 0-379-11387-2

Oceana's Legal Almanac Series: Law for the Layperson

ISSN 1075-7376

©2004 by Oceana Publications, Inc.

To My Husband Chris

Your love and support
are my motivation and inspiration

-and-

In memory of my son, Jimmy

Table of Contents

CHAPTER 3:
THE SOCIAL SECURITY CARD

CHAPTER 4:
SOCIAL SECURITY FUNDING

CHAPTER 5:
THE SOCIAL SECURITY
RETIREMENT PENSION

CHAPTER 6:
SOCIAL SECURITY DISABILITY INSURANCE

CHAPTER 7:
SURVIVORS BENEFITS

CHAPTER 10:
REPRESENTATIVE PAYEES

CHAPTER 11:
THE CLAIMANT'S RIGHT
TO REPRESENTATION

ABOUT THE AUTHOR

MARGARET C. JASPER is an attorney engaged in the general practice of law in South Salem, New York, concentrating in the areas of personal injury and entertainment law. Ms. Jasper holds a Juris Doctor degree from Pace University School of Law, White Plains, New York, is a member of the New York and Connecticut bars, and is certified to practice before the United States District Courts for the Southern and Eastern Districts of New York, the United States Court of Appeals for the Second Circuit, and the United States Supreme Court.

Ms. Jasper has been appointed to the panel of arbitrators of the American Arbitration Association and the law guardian panel for the Family Court of the State of New York, is a member of the Association of Trial Lawyers of America, and is a New York State licensed real estate broker and member of the Westchester County Board of Realtors, operating as Jasper Real Estate, in South Salem, New York. She maintains a website at http://www.JasperLawOffice.com.

Ms. Jasper is the author and general editor of the following legal almanacs: AIDS Law; The Americans with Disabilities Act; Animal Rights Law; The Law of Attachment and Garnishment; Bankruptcy Law for the Individual Debtor; Individual Bankruptcy and Restructuring; Banks and their Customers; Buying and Selling Your Home; The Law of Buying and Selling; The Law of Capital Punishment; The Law of Child Custody; Commercial Law; Consumer Rights Law; The Law of Contracts; Copyright Law; Credit Cards and the Law; The Law of Debt Collection; Dictionary of Selected Legal Terms; The Law of Dispute Resolution; The Law of Drunk Driving; DWI, DUI and the Law; Education Law; Elder Law; Employee Rights in the Workplace; Employment Discrimination Under Title VII; Environmental Law; Estate Planning; Everyday Legal Forms; Executors and Personal Representatives: Rights and Responsibilities; Harassment in the Workplace; Health Care and Your Rights. Home Mortgage Law Primer; Hospital Liability

Law; Identity Theft and How To Protect Yourself; Insurance Law; The Law of Immigration; International Adoption; Juvenile Justice and Children's Law; Labor Law; Landlord-Tenant Law; The Law of Libel and Slander; Living Together: Practical Legal Issues; Marriage and Divorce; The Law of Medical Malpractice; Motor Vehicle Law; The Law of No-Fault Insurance; Nursing Home Negligence; The Law of Obscenity and Pornography; Patent Law; The Law of Personal Injury; Privacy and the Internet: Your Rights and Expectations Under the Law; Probate Law; The Law of Product Liability; Real Estate Law for the Homeowner and Broker; Religion and the Law; Retirement Planning; The Right to Die; Law for the Small Business Owner; Social Security Law; Special Education Law; The Law of Speech and the First Amendment; Teenagers and Substance Abuse; Trademark Law; Victim's Rights Law; The Law of Violence Against Women; Welfare: Your Rights and the Law; What if it Happened to You: Violent Crimes and Victims' Rights; What if the Product Doesn't Work: Warranties & Guarantees; Workers' Compensation Law; and Your Child's Legal Rights: An Overview.

INTRODUCTION

A fact of life which society cannot ignore is the financial dependence of its aging and disabled population. The social security system is concerned with providing disadvantaged people with economic security, particularly when they reach the age where they are no longer able to work to support themselves, or are otherwise disabled and unable to earn a living.

The traditional sources of economic security include one's assets; income and pension; family resources; and charitable organizations. Unfortunately, one or more of these sources of economic security are not always available to everyone in need, and people look to their government for assistance.

The social security system is a statutory creation. The Social Security Act of 1934 was passed primarily to provide a retirement pension program for senior citizens and assist disabled individuals. Over the past 60 years, the social security system has become an essential component of modern American life. It addresses the needs of those whose economic security is threatened by events such as unemployment, illness, disability, death, and old age.

One in seven Americans receives some type of social security benefit. More than 90 percent of all workers are in jobs covered by social security. In 1940, approximately 222,000 people received monthly social security benefits. Today, benefits are distributed to over 42 million Americans.

This almanac explores the history of the legislation and early administration of the social security system, the establishment of the Social Security Administration (SSA), the manner in which the social security system is funded and wages are recorded, and the distribution of social security numbers and cards. This almanac also discusses the individual programs administered by the SSA, such as retirement pension benefits, medicare, supplemental security income, survivor benefits, and disability benefits, including application information, and eligibility and benefit issues.

The Appendix provides sample forms and documents, and other pertinent information and data. The Glossary contains definitions of many of the terms used throughout the almanac.

CHAPTER 1:
HISTORY AND DEVELOPMENT OF
SOCIAL INSURANCE

THE ENGLISH MODEL

In the Middle Ages, European society recognized that economic security could be obtained by the formation of formal organizations which protected their members. The earliest of such organizations were the merchant and craftsmen guilds. These guilds were formed by individuals who had a common trade or business.

In addition to regulating production and employment, these organizations provided benefits—e.g., financial assistance and death benefits—to their members in time of need. These guilds evolved into what were known as fraternal organizations—forerunners of the modern trade unions—which began the practice of offering life insurance to members. Following the Industrial Revolution, these types of organizations flourished and, by the early 19th century, one in nine men belonged to such an organization. In fact, early American settlers continued the establishment of fraternal organizations in the American colonies.

The English "Poor Laws"

As the government stepped in and began to assume responsibility for its citizens' economic security, a series of *Poor Laws* were adopted to help the disadvantaged. The *English Poor Law of 1601* was the first statute which dealt with the government's responsibility to provide for the welfare of its people. Under this statute, taxes were assessed to fund relief programs which were locally controlled, and *almshouses* were founded to shelter the homeless.

Although the law acknowledged the government's responsibility for the needy, it was also considered harsh in that it viewed the poor as undesirables and treated them likewise. In addition, amongst the poor, there were distinctions made as to which individuals were deserving of aid and which individuals were ineligible.

AMERICAN COLONIES

When the English-speaking colonists arrived in America, they established *Poor Laws* similar to those they were accustomed to in England. The early colonial laws also used taxation as a means to fund the programs, which were again administered locally. The colonies also distinguished between poor persons who were deemed "worthy" of assistance, and those who were not eligible for relief.

As the colonies expanded, local control over financial aid to the poor became burdensome, and state assistance was sought. Through the 18th and 19th centuries, "almshouses" and "poorhouses" were instituted to shelter and provide relief to the indigent population. However, obtaining such relief was purposely made very difficult in order to discourage dependency on the state. For example, personal property could be forfeited, as well as the right to vote and freely move throughout society. In some cases, those receiving assistance were required to display certain markings on their clothing.

Distributing financial assistance outside of the poorhouses was frowned upon because the citizens did not want to encourage dependency on the state by making it easier to obtain help. However, operating the poorhouses became increasingly expensive, and some financial assistance outside of the poorhouse setting began to occur. Nevertheless, society sought to keep government assistance in this area to a bare minimum.

THE CIVIL WAR PERIOD

The Civil War resulted in hundreds of thousands of disabled veterans, widows and orphans. During that time, the dependent American population was proportionally the largest it has ever been in history. In response to this crisis, a pension program, with many similarities to our current social security system, was developed.

The first piece of legislation was passed in 1862, and provided pension benefits to soldiers who were disabled as a result of their military duty. Widows and orphans were eligible for pension benefits that their parent or spouse would have received had they been disabled. Nevertheless, former Confederate soldiers and their families were barred from receiving Civil War pensions.

By 1890, a military service connected disability was no longer required, thus any disabled Civil War veteran was eligible for benefits and, by 1906, Civil War pension benefits were extended to older Americans. Nevertheless, this forerunner of the modern social security system was not extended to the general population until much later.

THE INDUSTRIAL REVOLUTION

The deterioration of the traditional sources of economic security in America was attributed to cultural and demographic changes which began with the Industrial Revolution. The Industrial Revolution transformed a largely agricultural society to a nation of industrial workers. Thus, individuals could no longer depend on their own hard work to put a meal on the table for their family, but were subject to conditions outside of their control, such as the possibility of unemployment.

In addition, the change from an agricultural society to an industrial society forced many Americans to move from farms to urban areas, and largely accounted for the subsequent disappearance of the extended family—i.e., a household which included grandparents and other relatives. The extended family was beneficial in that the family assumed financial responsibility for any members who became disabled or too old to work.

Another significant and related demographic change which developed was the increase in life expectancy due, in large part, to advances in public health care. As a result, there was a rapid growth in the elderly population, and there were no programs in place to address this growing problem.

THE DEPRESSION ERA

In the 1920s, it was not just the wealthy who invested their fortunes in the stock market. There were many smaller investors who gambled their modest incomes in a system that promised them riches. When the stock market crashed on October 24, 1929, the economic security of millions of Americans disappeared overnight and America slipped into an economic Depression.

In the 1930s, America's economy was in crisis. Unemployment was at a record level, banks and businesses were failing, and the majority of the elderly population lived in poverty. Prior to the 1930s, there were virtually no state welfare pensions for the elderly. In response to changing demographics and the growing economic crisis, approximately 30 states passed some form of old-age welfare pension program by 1935. However, benefits under these programs were modest, eligibility was restricted based on income, and many of the programs were inadequately implemented.

There was a public outcry for a federal response to this growing problem, and a number of movements developed each with a proposed pension scheme. President Herbert Hoover responded that the most effective way to combat economic insecurity was through voluntary relief. Hoover had enjoyed success in international relief efforts, before and after World War I, through the efforts of voluntary partnerships of government, business and private donations.

Hoover believed this kind of "volunteerism" would solve the problems of the Depression. Although he authorized some limited federal relief efforts, his main response to the Depression was to advocate these voluntary efforts. Unfortunately, voluntary charity proved impossible because the nation's wealth had been so profoundly diminished in the three years following the stock market crash.

THE CONCEPT OF SOCIAL INSURANCE - THE ROOSEVELT ADMINISTRATION

President Franklin D. Roosevelt introduced an economic security proposal based on social insurance rather than welfare assistance to address the permanent problem of economic security for the elderly. Social insurance programs had been successfully implemented in many European countries since the 19th century.

Social insurance endeavors to solve the problem of threatened economic security by pooling risk assets from a large social group and providing income to those members of the group whose economic security is imperiled, e.g., by unemployment, disability, or cessation of work due to old age.

Under Roosevelt's proposal, a work-related, contributory system would be created in which workers would provide for their own future economic security through taxes paid while employed. The Social Security program that was eventually adopted in late 1935 relied on this concept of "social insurance."

THE SOCIAL SECURITY ACT OF 1935

The Social Security Act was signed by President Roosevelt on August 14, 1935. Originally, the Social Security Act was named the Economic Security Act, but this title was changed during Congressional consideration of the bill. Taxes were collected for the first time in January 1937 and the first one-time lump-sum payments were made that same month.

One-time lump-sum payments were the only form of benefits paid during the start-up period beginning January 1937 through December 1939. The earliest reported recipient of a lump-sum benefit was a retired Cleveland motorman named Ernest Ackerman. Mr. Ackerman retired one day after the Social Security program began. During his one day of participation in the program, a nickel was withheld from Mr. Ackerman's pay for Social Security. Upon his retirement, Mr. Ackerman received a lump-sum payment of 17 cents.

Regular ongoing monthly benefits started in January 1940. On January 31, 1940, the first monthly Social Security retirement check was issued to Ida May Fuller of Ludlow, Vermont, in the amount of $22.54. Miss Fuller died in January 1975 at the age of 100. During her 35 years as a beneficiary, she received over $22,000 in benefits.

Under the 1935 law, Social Security only paid retirement benefits to the primary worker. A 1939 change in the law added survivors benefits and benefits for the retiree's spouse and children. Disability benefits were added in 1956.

ORGANIZATION OF THE SOCIAL SECURITY ADMINISTRATION

The Social Security Act of 1935 established the three-member *Social Security Board* to administer the programs established by the Act, which included social security, unemployment compensation and various public assistance programs. The Board then established the *Bureau of Federal Old-Age Insurance*—subsequently renamed the *Bureau of Old-Age and Survivors Insurance*—as the agency responsible for administering social security benefits.

In 1946, the Social Security Board was abolished and the Social Security Administration (SSA) was established. In 1963, a Welfare Administration was established to administer the public assistance programs, leaving social security to the Social Security Administration and marking the end of the Bureau of Old-Age and Survivors Insurance.

The Social Security Board, and the subsequent Social Security Administration, were under the jurisdiction of the Federal Security Agency from 1939 to 1953, when the Department of Health, Education, and Welfare—subsequently renamed the *Department of Health and Human Services*—was established and designated the SSA's parent organization.

Throughout the 1980s and 1990s, there was growing bipartisan support for removing the SSA from under the Department of Health and Human Services, and establishing it as an independent agency. In 1994, the Social Security Independence and Program Improvements Act of 1994 (P.L. 103-296) was passed unanimously by Congress and, on August 14, 1994, President Bill Clinton signed the Act into law. The SSA now operates as an independent agency.

A directory of Social Security Administration Regional Offices is set forth at Appendix 1.

MODERN DAY SOCIAL SECURITY

Social Security is now known as *Old Age, Survivors and Disability Insurance (OASDI)* under Title II of the Social Security Act. It is a national program created by Congress, which pays money to retirees, survivors of deceased workers, and people who have become disabled. Although there are a variety of benefits paid out under the social security program, social security commonly refers to money paid to older workers or retirees who have made contributions to the program from their earned income. Most employees are required to contribute, though some state and local government workers are exempt.

From the beginning, it was recognized that the provision of old-age annuities for some 30 to 40 million men and women was clearly a massive undertaking never before attempted by the Federal Government. Administratively, old-age insurance loomed up as the leviathan of the Social Security Act. Unlike unemployment compensation programs and public assistance programs, which are administered jointly by the Federal Government with assistance by the state governments, the administration of old-age insurance is a responsibility assumed by the Federal Government alone. Though consideration of state laws enters into one aspect of old-age insurance, administration of this program is comparatively simple. Most of its problems arise from its size.

The concept of "retirement" after a long period of working years was not always available to the elderly before the social security system was developed. When the Social Security retirement benefits program was instituted, it was not intended to provide a comfortable standard of living in retirement, but to supplement income, including personal savings and pension benefits. Unfortunately, many senior citizens are now trying to live out their retirement years dependent solely on their Social Security checks. This may be due to the fact that their former employment did not provide a pension, or because they did not save any money during their working years to supplement their social security income.

STATISTICS

An estimated 156 million workers, 96% of all workers, are covered under Social Security:

Elderly and Retired Recipients

Social Security is the major source of income for most of the elderly:

In 1940, the life expectancy of a 65-year-old was 12-1/2 years, today it's 17-1/2 years.

Currently, 53% of the workforce has no private pension coverage, and 32% of the workforce has no savings set aside specifically for retirement.

Nine out of ten individuals age 65 and older receive Social Security benefits.

Social Security benefits represent 39% of income of the elderly.

About two-thirds of aged Social Security beneficiaries receive 50% or more of their income from Social Security.

Social Security is the only source of income for approximately 22% of the elderly.

Retired workers and their dependents account for 69% of total benefits paid.

Disabled Workers

Social Security is also a source of income for disabled workers:

Almost 3 in 10 of today's 20 year-olds will become disabled before reaching age 67.

Disabled workers and their dependents account for 16% of total benefits paid.

About ninety percent of workers age 21-64 in covered employment and their families have protection in the event of a long-term disability.

72% of the private sector workforce has no long-term disability insurance.

Survivors Benefits

Social Security provides some security for the survivors of deceased workers:

One in seven Americans will die before reaching age 67.

Survivors of deceased workers account for 15% of total benefits paid.

An estimated 97% of young children and their mothers and fathers are insured for survivors benefits through Social Security.

Distribution of Benefits—2003

In 2003, nearly 47 million Americans received approximately $470 billion in Social Security benefits, allocated as follows:

Approximately 29.5 billion retired workers received a total of $27.2 billion dollars, with an average monthly benefit of $922.00, and approximately 3.1 million of their dependents received $1.4 billion dollars.

Approximately 5.9 million disabled workers received $5 billion dollars, with an average monthly benefit of $862.00, and approximately 1.7 million of their dependents received $.4 billion dollars.

Approximately 6.8 million survivors received $5.3 billion dollars, with an average monthly benefit of $888.00.

Future Recipients

The future of Social Security is a major concern:

By 2030, there will be twice as many older Americans as today—from 36 million today to 70 million in 2030.

There are currently 3.3 workers for each Social Security beneficiary. By 2030, there will be 2.2 workers for each beneficiary.

CHAPTER 2:
THE SOCIAL SECURITY NUMBER

HISTORY OF THE SOCIAL SECURITY NUMBER

Following the enactment of the Social Security Act of 1935, the Social Security Board was faced with the enormous task of registering workers so that they could begin earning credits toward old-age benefits by January 1, 1937.

The Social Security Board had to devise a system whereby each worker could be identified and connected with the wages reported by his or her employer so that there would be a complete and accurate record to use in order to compute the worker's benefits. Using names and addresses as a means of identification was ruled out because many thousands of workers had identical names, and addresses would only have short-term usage. Another means of positive identification was necessary.

It was finally decided that each covered individual would be assigned an account number, and personal information would be obtained for permanent association between the individual and the account number. This personal information, supplied by the worker when applying for an account number, included: (i) name and address; (ii) employer's name and address at the time the application is filed; (iii) age and date of birth; (iv) place of birth; (v) father's full name; (vi) mother's maiden name; (vii) sex; (viii) color; and (ix) signature.

The assignment of a social security number (SSN) to each individual worker in covered employment was begun in November 1936. However, because the newly-formed Social Security Board did not have sufficient resources, they contracted with the U.S. Postal Service to accomplish the registration process.

The local post offices distributed the applications and assigned the social security numbers. The post offices then collected the completed forms and turned them over to the Social Security field offices located near major post office centers. The applications were forwarded to Baltimore, Maryland, where the social security numbers were registered and various employment records established. The process of issuing social security numbers is called *enumeration*.

With the assistance of the post offices, over 30 million social security numbers were issued through this early registration procedure. In addition, more than 2.6 million identification numbers were assigned to employers. By June 30, 1937, the Social Security Board had established 151 field offices and was able to take over the responsibility of assigning social security numbers. By the end of March 1938, applications for account numbers totaled more than 38 million.

Today the issuance of social security numbers is essentially a fully automated process. This process is known as the *Automated Enumeration Screening Process*. The field offices receive the applications, verify the identity proofs, and electronically transmit the information from the application to the Central Office for assignment of a number. In the Central Office the information is checked by computer against information already on file to determine whether the application duplicates an earlier application. If so, a duplicate card is issued. Otherwise, unless there are discrepancies, a new social security number is assigned and a new card is issued.

The original application, which is retained for a short period of time in the field office, is later sent to a records center in Pennsylvania for microfilming and filing. The original document is destroyed once the microfilm has been made. If the original document is needed for a signature verification or fraud investigation, a microprint is produced from the film.

According to the Social Security Administration, approximately 381 million social security numbers have been assigned as of 1996.

A table of total social security numbers issued by calendar year (1936-1996) is set forth at Appendix 2.

MEANING OF THE SOCIAL SECURITY NUMBER

The social security account number is composed of nine digits, divided into three sections. The first three digits specify a geographical area, the next two indicate a group, and the remaining four specify an individual serial number. The United States, Alaska, and Hawaii are divided into approximately 380 different administrative areas, each with a different number.

The Area Number

The area number, which is represented by the first three digits, is determined by the geographical area in which the individual resided at the time he or she registered. Generally, area numbers were assigned beginning in the northeast and moving westward. Thus, people on the east coast have the lowest numbers and those on the west coast have the highest numbers.

A table listing social security area numbers by geographical region is set forth at Appendix 3.

The Group Number

The group number, indicated by the two middle digits, was determined by the procedure of issuing numbers in groups of 10,000 to post offices for assignment at the beginning of the enumeration. The group number no longer has any geographic or data significance but merely serves to break the number into conveniently sized blocks for orderly issuance.

The Serial Number

The last four digits represent the serial number. The serial numbers represent a straight numerical sequence of digits from 0001-9999 within the group.

Because the 9-digit social security number allows for about 1 billion possible combinations, and only 390 million have been issued to date, the Social Security Administration does not expect to have to recycle old numbers for quite some time. Thus, when an individual dies, their number is not reissued to another person. The decedent's social security number is simply removed from the active files and is not reused.

SOCIAL SECURITY NUMBER AS IDENTIFICATION

The initial registration only assigned social security numbers to adults who were working in covered employment. Over the years, the social security number has become widely used for purposes not associated with the social security program. Many governments, schools, businesses, and financial institutions use an individual's social security number for client identification and record-keeping purposes.

As a result, the average age of applicants has dropped considerably. Currently, about 94 percent of all applicants are under age 22; 74 percent are under age 15; and 41 percent are under age 5, the majority of which are under age 2.

Although obtaining a social security number for a newborn is strictly voluntary, the Social Security Administration urges parents to obtain a social security number for their newborns at birth for a number of reasons. For example, any child claimed on a taxpayer's income tax return must have a social security number. In addition, children generally need their own social security number if a bank account will be opened for them, or savings bonds purchased for them. Social security numbers for children may also be needed to obtain medical coverage or apply for various types of government services.

A parent may request a social security number for a newborn at the time the hospital representative requests information for the baby's birth certificate, and a social security card will be processed. If the social security number is not requested at the hospital, one may be obtained later by contacting the local Social Security office and filing the necessary papers.

CHRONOLOGY OF LEGISLATION AFFECTING THE USE OF THE SOCIAL SECURITY NUMBER (1937-1998)

In 1935, The Social Security Act (P.L. 74-271) was enacted. Although it did not expressly mention the use of social security numbers, it authorized the creation of some type of record-keeping scheme.

In 1936, Treasury Decision 4704 required the issuance of an account number to each employee covered by the Social Security program.

In 1943, Executive Order 9397 required: (i) all Federal components to use the social security number "exclusively" whenever the component found it advisable to set up a new identification system for individuals; and (ii) the Social Security Board to cooperate with Federal uses of the number by issuing and verifying numbers for other Federal agencies.

In 1961, the Civil Service Commission adopted the SSN as an official Federal employee identifier.

In 1961, the Internal Revenue Code Amendments (P.L. 87-397) required each taxpayer to furnish an identifying number for tax reporting.

In 1962, the Internal Revenue Service adopted the social security number as its official taxpayer identification number.

In 1964, the Treasury Department, via internal policy, required buyers of Series H savings bonds to provide their social security numbers.

In 1965, the Internal Revenue Amendments (P.L. 89-384) enacted Medicare. It became necessary for most individuals age 65 and older to have a social security number.

In 1966, the Veterans Administration began to use the social security number as the hospital admissions number and for patient record-keeping.

In 1967, the Department of Defense adopted the social security number in lieu of the military service number for identifying Armed Forces personnel.

In 1970, the Bank Records and Foreign Transactions Act (P.L. 91-508) required all banks, savings and loan associations, credit unions, and brokers/dealers in securities to obtain the social security numbers of all of their customers. Also, financial institutions were required to file a report with the IRS, including the social security number of the customer, for any transaction involving more than $10,000.

In 1971, an SSA task force report was published which proposed that the SSA take a "cautious and conservative" position toward social security number use and do nothing to promote the use of the social security number as an identifier. The report also recommended that the SSA use mass social security number enumeration in schools as a long-range, cost-effective approach to tightening up the social security number system, and consider cooperating with specific health, education and welfare uses of the social security number by State, local, and other nonprofit organizations.

In 1972, the Social Security Amendments of 1972 (P.L. 92-603): (i) required the SSA to issue social security numbers to all legally admitted aliens upon entry, and to anyone receiving or applying for any benefit paid for by Federal funds; (ii) required the SSA to obtain evidence to establish age, citizenship, or alien status and identity; and (iii) authorized the SSA to enumerate children at the time they first entered school.

In 1973, buyers of series E savings bonds were required by the Treasury Department to provide their social security numbers.

In 1973, a report of the HEW Secretary's Advisory Committee on Automated Personal Data System concluded that the adoption of a universal identifier by this country was not desirable; and also found that the social security number was not suitable for such a purpose as it does not meet the criteria of a universal identifier that distinguishes a person from all others.

In 1974, the Privacy Act (P.L. 93-579) was enacted, effective September 27, 1975, to limit governmental use of the social security number and: (i) provided that no State or local government agency may withhold a benefit from a person simply because the individual refuses to furnish his or her social security number; and (ii) required that Federal, State and local agencies which request an individual to disclose his or her social security number inform the individual if disclosure was mandatory or voluntary.

In 1975, the Social Services Amendments of 1974 (P.L. 93-647) provided that: (i) disclosure of an individual's social security number is a condition of eligibility for AFDC benefits; and (ii) the Office of Child Support Enforcement Parent Locator Service may require disclosure of limited information, including social security number and whereabouts, contained in SSA records.

In 1976, under the Tax Reform Act of 1976 (P.L. 94-455), amendments were made to the Social Security Act to: (i) allow use by the States of the social security number in the administration of any tax, general public assistance, driver's license or motor vehicle registration law within their jurisdiction and to authorize the States to require individuals affected by such laws to furnish their social security numbers to the States; (ii) make misuse of the social security number for any purpose a violation of the Social Security Act; (iii) make disclosure or compelling disclosure of the social security number of any person a violation of the Social Security Act; and (iv) amend section 6109 of the Internal Revenue Code to provide that the social security number be used as the tax identification number (TIN) for all tax purposes. While the Treasury Department had been using the social security number as the TIN by regulation since 1962, this law codified that requirement.

In 1976, the Federal Advisory Committee on False Identification: (i) recommended that penalties for misuse should be increased and evidence requirements tightened; and (ii) rejected the idea of a national identifier and would not consider the social security number for such a purpose.

In 1977, the Food Stamp Act of 1977 (P.L. 96-58) required disclosure of social security numbers of all household members as a condition of eligibility for participation in the food stamp program.

In 1977, a Privacy Protection Study Commission recommended that: (i) no steps be taken towards developing a standard, universal label for individuals until safeguards and policies regarding permissible uses and disclosures were proven effective; and (ii) Executive Order 9397 be amended so that Federal agencies could no longer use it as legal authority to require disclosure of an individual's social security number. However, no action was taken.

In 1978, the SSA required evidence of age, citizenship, and identity of all social security number applicants.

In 1981, the Omnibus Budget Reconciliation Act of 1981 (P.L. 97-35) required the disclosure of the social security numbers of all adult members in the household of children applying to the school lunch program.

In 1981, under the Social Security Benefits Act (P.L. 97-123): (i) Section 4 added alteration and forgery of a Social Security card to the list of prohibited acts and increased the penalties for such acts; and (ii) Section 6 required any Federal, State or local government agency to furnish the name and social security number of prisoners convicted of a felony to the Secretary of Health and Human Services, to enforce suspension of disability benefits to certain imprisoned felons.

In 1981, the Department of Defense Authorization Act (P.L. 97-86) required disclosure of the social security numbers to the Selective Service System of all individuals required to register for the draft.

In 1982, the Debt Collection Act (P.L. 97-365) required that all applicants for loans under any Federal loan program furnish their social security numbers to the agency supplying the loan.

In 1982, all social security cards issued to legal aliens not authorized to work within the United States were annotated "not valid for employment" beginning in May 1982.

In 1983, the Social Security Amendments of 1983 (P.L. 98-21) required that new and replacement Social Security cards issued after October 30th be made of banknote paper and, to the maximum extent practicable, not be subject to counterfeiting.

In 1983, the Interest and Dividend Tax Compliance Act (P.L. 98-67) required social security numbers for all interest-bearing accounts and provided a penalty of $50 for all individuals who fail to furnish a correct taxpayer identification number—usually the social security number.

In 1984, the Deficit Reduction Act of 1984 (P.L. 98-369): (i) amended the Social Security Act to establish an income and eligibility verification system involving State agencies administering the AFDC, Medicaid, unemployment compensation, the food stamp programs, and State programs under a plan approved under title I, X, XIV, or XVI of the Act and permitted states to require the social security number as a condition of eligibility for benefits under any of these programs; (ii) amended Section 60501 of the IRC to require that persons engaged in a trade or business file a report with the IRS, including social security numbers, for cash transactions over $10,000; and (iii) amended Section 215 of the IRC to authorize the Secretary of Health and Human Services to publish regulations that require a spouse paying alimony to furnish the IRS with the taxpayer identification number—i.e., the social security number—of the spouse receiving alimony payments.

In 1986, the Immigration Reform and Control Act of 1986 (P.L. 99-603): (i) required the Comptroller General to investigate technological changes that could reduce the potential for counterfeiting Social Security cards; (ii) provided that the Social Security card may be used to establish the eligibility of a prospective employee for employment; and (iii) required the Secretary of Health and Human Services to undertake a study of the feasibility and costs of establishing a social security number verification system.

In 1986, the Tax Reform Act of 1986 (P.L. 99-514) required individuals filing a tax return due after December 31, 1987 to include the taxpayer identification number—usually the social security number—of each dependent age 5 or older.

In 1986, the Commercial Motor Vehicle Safety Act of 1986 (P.L. 99-750) authorized the Secretary of Transportation to require the use of the social security number on commercial motor vehicle operators' licenses.

In 1986, the Higher Education Amendments of 1986 (P.L. 99-498) required that student loan applicants submit their social security number as a condition of eligibility.

In 1987, the SSA initiated a demonstration project on August 17th in the State of New Mexico enabling parents to obtain social security numbers for their newborn infants automatically when the infant's birth is registered by the State. The program was expanded nationwide in 1989. Currently, all 50 States participate in the program, as well as New York City, Washington, D.C., and Puerto Rico.

In 1988, the Housing and Community Development Act of 1987 (P.L. 100-242) authorized the Secretary of HUD to require disclosure of a person's social security number as a condition of eligibility for any HUD program.

In 1988, under The Family Support Act of 1988 (P.L. 100-485): (i) Section 125 required, beginning November 1, 1990, a State to obtain the social security numbers of the parents when issuing a birth certificate; and (ii) Section 704(a) required individuals filing a tax return due after December 31, 1989 to include the taxpayer identification number—usually the social security number—of each dependent age 2 or older.

In 1988, The Technical and Miscellaneous Revenue Act of 1988 (P.L. 100-647): (i) authorized a State and/or any blood donation facility to use social security numbers to identify blood donors (205(c)(2)(F)); and (ii) required that all Title II beneficiaries either have or have applied for a social security number in order to receive benefits. This provision became effective with dates of initial entitlement of June 1989 or later. Beneficiaries who refused enumeration were entitled but placed in suspense.

In 1988, the Anti-Drug Abuse Act of 1988 (P.L. 100-690) deleted the $5,000 and $25,000 upper limits on fines that can be imposed for violations of section 208 of the Social Security Act. The general limit of $250,000 for felonies in the U.S. Code now applied to social security number violations under section 208 of the Social Security Act.

In 1989, the Omnibus Budget Reconciliation Act of 1989 (P.L. 101-239) required that the National Student Loan Data System include, among other things, the names and social security numbers of borrowers.

In 1989, the Child Nutrition and WIC Reauthorization Act of 1989 (P.L. 101-147) required the member of the household who applies for the school lunch program to provide the social security number of the parent of the child for whom the application is made.

In 1990, under the Omnibus Budget Reconciliation Act of 1990 (P.L. 101-508): (i) Section 7201 (Computer Matching and Privacy Protection Amendments of 1990) provided that no adverse action may be taken against an individual receiving benefits as a result of a matching program without verification of the information or notification of the individual regarding the findings with time to contest; (ii) Section 8053, required a social security number for eligibility for benefits from the Department of Veterans Affairs (DVA); and (iii) Section 11112 required that individuals filing a tax return due after December 31, 1991, include the taxpayer identification number—usually the social security number—of each dependent age 1 or older.

In 1990, under the Food and Agricultural Resources Act of 1990 (P.L. 101-624), Section 1735: (i) required a social security number for the officers of food and retail stores that redeem food stamps; and (ii) provided that social security numbers maintained as a result of any law enacted on or after October 1, 1990, will be confidential and may not be disclosed.

In 1994, under the Social Security Independence and Program Improvements Act of 1994 (P.L. 103-296): (i) Section 304 authorized the use of the social security number for jury selection; (ii) Section 314 authorized cross-matching of social security numbers and Employer Identification Numbers maintained by the Department of Agriculture with other Federal agencies for the purpose of investigating both food stamp fraud and violations of other Federal laws; and (iii) Section 318 authorized the use of the social security number by the Department of Labor in administration of Federal workers' compensation laws.

In 1996, under the Personal Responsibility and Work Opportunity Reconciliation Act of 1996 (P.L. 104-193) (Welfare Reform): (i) Section 111 required the Commissioner of Social Security to develop and submit to Congress a prototype of a counterfeit-resistant Social Security card that: is made of durable, tamper-resistant material (e.g., plastic); employs technologies that provide security features (e.g., magnetic strip); and provides individuals with reliable proof of citizenship or legal resident alien status; (ii) Section 111 also required the Commissioner of Social Security to study and report to Congress on different methods of improving the Social Security card application process, including evaluation of the cost and workload implications of issuing a counterfeit-resistant Social Security card for all individuals and evaluation of the feasibility and cost implications of imposing a user fee for replacement cards; (iii) Section 316 required Health and Human Services to transmit to the SSA, for verification purposes, certain information about individuals and employers maintained under the Federal Parent Locator Service in an automated directory. The SSA is required to verify the accuracy of, correct, or supply to the extent possible, and report to Health and Human Services the name, social security number, and birth date of individuals and the employer identification number of employers. The SSA is to be reimbursed by Health and Human Services for the cost of this verification service. This section also required all Federal agencies, including the SSA, to report quarterly the name and social security number of each employee and the wages paid to the employee during the previous quarter; (iv) Section 317 provided that State child support enforcement procedures require the social security number of any applicant for a professional license, commercial driver's license, occupational license, or marriage license be recorded on the application. The social security number of any person subject to a divorce decree, support order, or paternity determination or acknowledgement would have to be placed in the pertinent records, and social security numbers are required on death certificates; and (v) Section 451 provides that, in order to be eligible for the Earned Income Tax Credit, an individual must include on his or her tax return a social security number which was not assigned solely for non-work purposes.

In 1997, under the Department of Defense Appropriations Act of 1997 (P.L. 104-208—Division C—Illegal Immigration Reform and Immigrant Responsibility Act of 1996): (i) Sections 401-404 provide for 3 specific employment verification pilot programs in which employers would voluntarily participate. In general, the pilot programs would allow an employer to confirm the identity and employment eligibility of the individual. The SSA and the Immigration and Naturalization Service (INS) would provide a secondary verification process to confirm the validity of the information provided. The SSA would compare the name and social security number provided and advise whether the name and number match SSA records and whether the social security number is valid for employment; (ii) Section 414 required the Commissioner to report to Congress every year, the aggregate number of social security numbers issued to noncitizens not authorized to work, but under which earnings were reported. This section also required the Commissioner to transmit to the Attorney General a report on the extent to which social security numbers and Social Security cards are used by noncitizens for fraudulent purposes; (iii) Section 415 authorized the Attorney General to require any noncitizen to provide his or her social security number for purposes of inclusion in any record maintained by the Attorney General or INS; (iv) Section 656 provided for improvements in identification-related documents; i.e., birth certificates and driver's licenses. These sections require publication of regulations which set standards, including security features and, in the case of driver's licenses, require that a social security number appear on the license. Federal agencies are precluded from accepting as proof of identity, documents which do not meet the regulatory standards; and (v) Section 657 provided for the development of a prototype Social Security card.

In 1997, under the Taxpayer Relief Act of 1997 (P.L. 105-34), Section 1090 required an applicant for a social security number under age 18 to provide evidence of his or her parents' names and social security numbers in addition to required evidence of age, identity, and citizenship.

In 1998, under The Omnibus Consolidated and Emergency Supplemental Appropriations Act of 1999 (P.L. 105-277): (i) Section 362 provides that no funds appropriated for the Department of Transportation (DOT) may be used to issue the final regulations required by Section 656(b) of the Illegal Immigration Reform and Responsibility Act of 1996; and (ii) Section 656(b) prohibits Federal agencies from accepting as proof of identification a drivers license that does not meet standards promulgated by the DOT. The standards include a document that contains a social security number that can be read electronically or visually and is in a form that includes security features to limit tampering and counterfeiting.

In 1998, the Identity Theft and Assumption Deterrence Act of 1998 (P.L. 105-318): (i) made identity theft—i.e., transferring or using another person's means of identification—a crime, subject to penalties. "Means of identification" includes another person's name, social security number, date of birth, official State or government issued driver's license or identification number, alien registration number, government passport number, and employer or taxpayer identification number; and (ii) established the Federal Trade Commission as a clearinghouse to receive complaints, provide informational materials to victims, and refer complaints to appropriate entities, which may include credit bureaus or law enforcement agencies.

In 1998, Vice President Gore announced a new policy to allow victims of domestic violence to change their social security number without proof that the abuser had misused their social security number.

In 1998, P.L. 105-379 amended the Food Stamp Act, effective June 1, 2000, to require: (i) each State agency that administers the food stamp program to enter into a cooperative arrangement with the Commissioner of Social Security under section 205(r) of the Social Security Act to verify whether food stamp recipients are deceased to ensure that benefits are not issued to deceased individuals; and (ii) the Secretary of Agriculture to report to Congress and to the Secretary of the Treasury on the progress and effectiveness of the cooperative arrangements established.

CHAPTER 3:
THE SOCIAL SECURITY CARD

HISTORY OF THE SOCIAL SECURITY CARD

Following the enactment of the Social Security Act of 1935, the Social Security Board considered a number of options in devising a social security identification card before it settled on the paper card that has been in existence for most of the past 50 years.

An initial proposal was to issue each worker a small metal plate upon which his or her name and number would be embossed, similar to a charge plate. This proposal had a number of advantages. The plate would be durable, and could be attached to a key ring to prevent loss. Employers could use its imprint to ensure an accurate record of the worker's social security number.

Nevertheless, this proposal was ultimately rejected because the plates could not be prepared in time to ensure completion of the initial enumeration by January 1, 1937. There was also public dissatisfaction in that the metal plates looked too much like military "dog tags" and were considered by many to signal excessive uniformity. The use of fingerprints to identify individuals for social security purposes was also rejected because there was such a strong association in the public mind between fingerprinting and criminality.

The Social Security Board also considered the possibility of attaching the worker's photograph to the card. However, this plan was discarded because it was too costly for the Government to photograph all workers. The Board also concluded that photographs would have to be updated over time.

In recent years, Congress has become concerned about the privacy of social security numbers due to their increasing use for non-social security related purposes, thus increasing the possibility of fraud. The Social Security Amendments of 1983 (Public Law 98-21) required that the social security card be made of banknote paper and, to the extent practicable, be counterfeit-proof. Beginning with cards issued on October 31, 1983, all new and replacement cards have met these criteria, marking the first substantial physical change in the card's appearance in 47 years.

TYPES OF SOCIAL SECURITY CARDS

The SSA issues three types of Social Security cards:

Unrestricted Employment

Most people have a Social Security card that simply has their name and Social Security number imprinted on the card. This card permits the holder to work without restriction. Unrestricted Social Security cards are issued to:

1. U.S. Citizens; or

2. People lawfully admitted to the United States with permanent Department of Homeland Security (DHS) work authorization.

Not Valid For Employment

The second type of card issued has an additional imprint on the card which reads: "Not Valid For Employment." This type of card is issued to:

1. People from other countries lawfully admitted to the United States who are not authorized to work by the DHS;

2. People who need a number because of a federal law requiring a Social Security number to get a benefit or service.

Valid For Work Only With DHS Authorization

The third type of card issued has an imprint which reads: "Valid For Work Only With INS Authorization." This type of card is issued to:

1. People lawfully admitted to the U.S. on a temporary basis; and

2. People who are authorized to work by the DHS.

APPLYING FOR A SOCIAL SECURITY CARD

Original Social Security Card

In order to obtain an original social security number and card, one must complete an Application for a Social Security Card (SSA Form SS-5). The application may be obtained in person at a local SSA office, by telephone (1-800-772-1313), or on the internet (www.socialsecurity.gov/online/ss-5.html). There is no application fee.

A sample Application for a Social Security Card (SSA Form SS-5) is attached at Appendix 4.

The application must be filed with the SSA along with at least two documents that can verify the applicant's age, identity, U.S. citizenship or lawful alien status, e.g. a birth certificate and a school record. It is advisable to contact the SSA by telephone and tell them what documents you intend to produce prior to filing the application in order to avoid having to refile if the documents produced are not acceptable. The SSA does not accept photocopies or notarized copies of documents. The applicant must submit original documents or copies certified by the custodian of the record.

Acceptable Proofs

Proof of Age

Proof of age can be shown by producing the original or a certified copy of the applicant's birth certificate. Other documents that the SSA may accept as proof of age include:

1. A hospital record of the applicant's birth created at the time of their birth;

2. A religious record showing the applicant's age made before they were 3 months old;

3. A passport;

4. An adoption record. The adoption record must indicate that the birth data was taken from the original birth certificate

Proof of Identity

As proof of identity, the SSA requires the applicant to produce a document in the name that the applicant wants shown on the card. The identity document must be of recent issuance. Preferably, the document should contain a photograph of the applicant, however, the SSA will generally accept a non-photo identity document if it contains enough identifying information, e.g., the applicant's name, as well as age, date of birth or parents' names. The SSA will not accept a birth certificate, hospital souvenir birth certificate, social security card or card stub, or social security record as evidence of identity. Documents that the SSA may accept as proof of identity include:

1. Driver's license;

2. Marriage or divorce record;

3. Military record;

4. Employee ID card;

5. Adoption record (only if not being used to establish age);

6. Life insurance policy;

7. Passport;

8. School ID card; or

9. Health insurance card (not a Medicare card).

In addition, as evidence of identity for infants and young children, the SSA may accept:

1. A doctor, clinic, or hospital record;

2. Daycare center or school record; or

3. Religious record, e.g., baptismal record.

Proof of U.S. Citizenship

As proof of U.S. citizenship, the SSA will accept most documents that show the applicant was born in the United States. If the applicant is a U.S. citizen born outside the United States, he or she must produce a U.S. consular report of birth; a U.S. Passport; a Certificate of Citizenship; or a Certificate of Naturalization.

Proof of Alien Status

As proof of alien status, the SSA requires production of an unexpired document issued to the applicant by the Department of Homeland Security (DHS) showing the applicant's immigration status (e.g., Form I-551, I-94, I-688B, or I-766). The SSA will not accept a receipt showing that the applicant applied for the document.

Submitting the Application for an Original Card

The application and original or certified documents may be mailed to or personally delivered to the applicant's local SSA office. The original documents will be returned immediately. The Social Security card is generally issued within two weeks of receiving the application.

If the applicant is age 12 or older, he or she must appear for an in-person interview. If the applicant was born in the United States, and is age 12 or older, he or she must be prepared to explain why they do not already have a Social Security number.

Replacement Social Security Card

Duplicate Card

In order to obtain a duplicate Social Security card when the holder's card has been lost or stolen, or a corrected card if the holder has changed their name, one must complete the Application for a Social Security Card (Form SS-5) referred to above, and produce evidence of their identity.

Corrected Card

In order to obtain a corrected card, the SSA requires the application to produce one or more documents which identify the applicant by both their old name as reflected in SSA records, and the applicant's new name, e.g., a marriage certificate, divorce decree, or a court order that changes the applicant's name. The SSA will also accept two identity documents—one in the applicant's old name and one in their new name. However, the SSA will not accept the applicant's old Social Security card as evidence of identity. The document showing the applicant's current identity must be recently issued.

Applicants Born Outside of the United States

Applicants for a duplicate or corrected card who were born outside of the United States must show proof of U.S. citizenship or lawful alien status.

Submitting the Application for a Replacement Card

Applicants for a replacement card must submit original or certified copies of the required documents. The application and original or certified documents may be mailed or personally delivered to the applicant's local SSA office. The original documents will be returned immediately.

The Social Security card is generally issued within two weeks of receiving the application. The duplicate card will have the same name and number as the original card. The corrected card will have the applicant's new name and the same number as the original card.

Applicants Living Outside the United States

Applicants for a Social Security card who are living outside the United States must complete and file a different form (Application for a Social Security Card (SS-5-FS)—Foreign Service).

LOST OR STOLEN SOCIAL SECURITY CARDS

If your Social Security card is lost or stolen, you should contact your local police department immediately to file a report. You should also contact the Social Security Administration to request a replacement Social Security card, as set forth above.

CHAPTER 4:
SOCIAL SECURITY FUNDING

IN GENERAL

Social Security is financed through a dedicated payroll tax. Employees, employers, and self-employed persons pay contributions, known as social security taxes, into the social security system during their working years. This tax deduction is generally designated as "FICA" on the employee's payroll stub.

The amount of these taxes, which is determined by Congress, is a percentage of one's gross salary, up to a designated limit. Employers pay social security taxes based on the employee's gross salary. For 2004, employers and employees each pay 6.2 percent of wages up to the current taxable maximum of $87,900, while the self-employed pay 12.4 percent.

Social Security taxes are used to pay for all Social Security benefits, including a portion of the Medicare insurance coverage. The money Social Security takes in generally exceeds the money it spends. The excess, called the "reserve," is pooled into special trust funds, known as the Social Security Trust Funds. The money in those trust funds is invested in Treasury bonds, which the government, by law, is required to pay back with interest.

THE FEDERAL INSURANCE CONTRIBUTIONS ACT (FICA)

Social Security payroll taxes are collected under the authority of the Federal Insurance Contributions Act (FICA), and generally referred to as *FICA taxes*. FICA was enacted following the Social Security Act of 1935.

In the original Act, the benefit provisions were contained in Title II and the taxing provisions were contained in Title VIII. The taxing provisions were contained in a separate Title for constitutional reasons. Under the 1939 amendments to Title VIII, the taxing provisions were removed from the Social Security Act and placed in the Internal Revenue Code (IRC). The new IRC section was then renamed the *Federal Insurance Contributions Act.*

This distinction was made because, although the payroll taxes collected for Social Security are indeed "taxes," they can also be characterized as "contributions" to the social insurance system. Thus, "FICA" now refers to the tax provisions of the Social Security Act, as contained in the Internal Revenue Code.

GENERAL REVENUE FUNDING

Social Security was designed to differ from welfare in that it was intended to be a self-supporting system rather than a government-subsidized system. Social Security is based on employee contributions, with the government acting as fund administrator rather than payer. For the most part, general tax revenues have never been used to support the Social Security system, except for the limited circumstances described below.

Military Personnel

Military service was not covered employment under the Social Security Act until 1957. Even though subsequently covered, a military salary is minimal compared to the private sector. Thus, a soldier's military earnings result in reduced social security benefits. In 1966, to address this disparity, Congress enacted legislation which granted military personnel special non-contributory wage credits for service before 1957, and special military wage credits to boost the amounts of credited contributions for service after 1956. These credits were paid out of general revenues as a subsidy to military personnel.

Prouty Benefits

In 1966, Congress also recognized that certain elderly individuals, who attained the age of 72 prior to 1968, had not been able to work long enough under the Social Security system to become eligible for benefits. These individuals were granted special Social Security benefits—known as "Special Age 72" or "Prouty" benefits—which were funded entirely by general revenues.

The Taxation of Social Security Benefits

As part of the 1983 Amendments, Social Security benefits became subject to federal income taxes for the first time. The funds generated by this new tax are returned to the Social Security Trust Funds from the general revenue.

SOCIAL SECURITY TRUST FUNDS

The first Federal Insurance Contributions Act (FICA) taxes were collected in January 1937. Special Trust Funds were created for these dedicated revenues, and benefits were paid from the monies in the Social Security Trust Funds. Over the years, more than $4.5 trillion has been paid into the Trust Funds, and more than $4.1 trillion has been paid out in benefits. The remainder is currently on reserve in the Trust Funds and will be used to pay future benefits.

There have been 11 years in which the Social Security program did not collect enough FICA taxes to pay the current year's benefits. During these years, Trust Fund bonds in the amount of about $24 billion made up the difference. In 1982, the Retirement Trust Fund borrowed some of the money from the Disability and Medicare Trust Funds. However, this money was fully repaid in 1986, and was the only time this type of "interfund borrowing" has occurred.

BENEFIT DISTRIBUTION

From 1937 until 1940, Social Security paid benefits in the form of a single, lump-sum payment. The purpose of these one-time lump sum payments was to provide some "payback" to those people who contributed to the program but would not participate long enough to be vested for monthly benefits. The average lump-sum payment during this period was $58.06.

Under the 1935 law, monthly benefits were to begin in 1942. The period between 1937 and 1942 was intended to both build up the Trust Funds and to provide a minimum period for participation in order to qualify for monthly benefits.

THE SOCIAL SECURITY STATEMENT

The Social Security Statement is a concise, easy-to-read personal record of the earnings on which an individual has paid Social Security taxes during their working years, and a summary of the estimated benefits the individual and his or her family may receive in the future as a result of those earnings.

An individual's Earning Statement does not include information about benefits they may be entitled to on anyone else's records, e.g. a spouse. To determine whether you qualify for benefits on another record, you must contact the SSA in writing, in person at the local SSA office, or by telephone (1-800-772-1213).

It is important to review one's Social Security Statement on a regular basis, for a number of important reasons, as set forth below.

First, one should use the information contained in the Statement to make sure that their reported earnings and identifying information, such as their name, date of birth and social security number, are correct on the record. Undetected errors on the Statement can result in a loss of Social Security benefits one is entitled to receive. Errors in the earnings record are more likely to occur if the individual changes jobs frequently or has more than one employer. If there are any errors in the report, one should contact the SSA and provide proof of their actual earnings, such as their W-2 forms, pay stubs, and tax returns. Regularly reviewing the Statement will make it easier to identify mistakes and have them corrected as soon as possible.

The Social Security Statement is also an important tool for financial planning. Information contained in one's Social Security Statement can assist an individual in planning their financial future and assessing what additional financial needs one may have upon retirement.

In addition, the general information contained in the Statement advises workers of all of the types of financial protection they are entitled to receive. For example, many people believe that Social Security is only a retirement program available to those who have reached retirement age. The Statement contains information on benefits available to younger workers in case of death or disability prior to reaching retirement age.

Requesting a Social Security Statement

The SSA distributes Social Security Statements in automatic annual mailings to workers and former workers aged 25 and older, approximately 3 months prior to the worker's birthdate. The SSA will also send a copy of the Statement at any time to workers of any age who request them. To request an earnings record, one must complete and submit a form entitled Request For Personal Earnings And Benefit Estimate Statement (SSA Form 7004). It takes approximately two to four weeks to receive a statement.

In order to receive a Statement, one must provide the SSA with the following information:

1. Name as shown on their Social Security Card;

2. Social Security Number;

3. Date of birth;

4. Place of birth; and

5. Mother's maiden name—last name only (to help in identification process).

According to the SSA, in order to obtain a better estimate of future benefits, the worker may optionally provide the SSA with (1) their last years' earnings and an estimate of their current and future earnings; and (2) the age at which the worker plans to stop working.

A copy of the Request for Earnings and Benefit Estimate Statement (Form SSA-7004) is set forth at Appendix 5.

CHAPTER 5:
THE SOCIAL SECURITY
RETIREMENT PENSION

IN GENERAL

During an individual's working years, they are required to contribute to the Social Security system through FICA taxes. When that person retires, the Social Security Administration pays the retiree a monthly benefit. The system is designed to work like a pension plan. The majority of Social Security recipients—approximately 60%—receive Social Security retirement benefits due to retirement. As of December 31, 2003, about 91 percent of the population aged 65 and over were receiving benefits.

A table setting forth the number of retired workers and their dependents receiving benefits (1970-2003)is set forth at Appendix 6.

DETERMINING THE RETIREMENT AGE

In 1889, Germany was the first nation to adopt an old-age social insurance program. Germany initially set age 70 as the retirement age but, in 1916, lowered that age to 65. When America moved to social insurance in 1935, the German system was still using age 65 as its retirement age. It is a long-held belief that this was a factor in determining 65 as America's designated retirement age.

However, according to the Committee on Economic Security (CES), America's decision instead stemmed from two sources: (i) the prevailing retirement ages in the few private pension systems in existence at the time and; (ii) the 30 state old-age pension systems then in operation, half of which used 65 as the retirement age. In addition, the federal Railroad Retirement System passed by Congress earlier in 1934 also used age 65 as its retirement age. Based on this information, the CES decided on age 65 as the retirement age for Social Security purposes. This decision was also confirmed by the actuarial studies which showed that using age 65 produced a manageable system that could easily be made self-sustaining with only modest levels of payroll taxation.

Nevertheless, as life expectancy increases, and the baby boom generation reaches senior citizenship, the SSA has foreseen the need to increase the eligibility age of retirees in future years. For example, Americans aged 65 or older comprised only 6.7% of the population in 1930 whereas, as of 1990, this segment of the population has expanded to 31.9%.

A life expectancy table depicting the remaining years of life based on age as of 1996 is set forth at Appendix 7.

Life expectancy at birth in 1930 was only 58 for men and 62 for women. Thus, there was much concern that, based on one's life expectancy at that time, Social Security was designed so that people would work for many years paying social security taxes, but would not live long enough to collect benefits.

Nevertheless, although life expectancy at birth was indeed less than 65, life expectancy as measured after the attainment of adulthood demonstrated that most Americans could expect to live to age 65 once they survived childhood. There was a low life expectancy at birth in the early decades of the 20th century caused by high infant mortality. Obviously, someone who died as a child would never have worked and paid into Social Security. Thus, the actuarial tables demonstrated that a more appropriate measure is life expectancy after attainment of adulthood.

For example, in 1940, almost 54% of men could expect to live to age 65 if they survived to age 21, and men who attained age 65 could expect to collect Social Security benefits for almost 13 years. These numbers were even higher for women. As of 1990, over 80% of those who survived to age 21 could expect to live to age 65, and those who attained the age of 65 could expect to collect benefits for almost 20 years.

A table setting forth the average remaining life expectancy of individuals who survive to age 65 (1940-1990) is set forth at Appendix 8.

ELIGIBILITY

As set forth above, the SSA has set age 65 as the retirement age for a person who was born before 1938 to receive full social security retirement benefits (known as "full retirement age"). Beginning in the year 2000, the age at which a person's full retirement benefits are payable started to increase gradually. For example, those born in 1940 reach "full retirement age" at 65 and 6 months. Individuals born in 1950, reach full retirement age at 66. Anybody born in 1960 or later will not be eligible for full retirement benefits until age 67.

A table depicting the eligibility age for full social security benefits according to year of birth is set forth at Appendix 9.

There are additional eligibility requirements for Social Security. For example, you must have worked for a specified number of years before you are eligible to receive Social Security retirement benefits. The amount of your monthly Social Security benefits is calculated according to a specified formula based on your average earnings over those employment years. Your earnings are tracked according to your Social Security number, which you are required to have if you are working. In fact, the Internal Revenue Service requires that a Social Security number be shown on tax returns for all dependents over the age of one.

As you work and pay Social Security taxes, you earn Social Security "credits," up to a maximum of four credits per year. The amount of money you need to earn one credit goes up each year. Currently, most people need 40 credits to qualify for benefits. Retirement benefits are calculated on earnings during a lifetime of work. During your lifetime, you will probably earn more credits than you need to be eligible for Social Security. However, it is your income, not the number of credits you earn, that determines the amount of your benefit under the Social Security system. Years of high earnings will increase the amount of the benefit. Because benefit computations are based on a person's date of birth and complete work history, there are differences in amounts among recipients.

In most cases, Social Security retirement benefits do not begin the month the person reaches the age of eligibility. Benefits usually begin the following month. To receive retirement benefits, you must have attained the age of eligibility for the entire month. Nevertheless, the law provides that one "attains" their age the day before their birthday. Thus, individuals born on the 1st or 2nd day of the month will usually be eligible for benefits beginning the month of their birth.

FAMILY BENEFITS

When an individual becomes eligible for retirement benefits, certain family members may also be entitled to receive benefits. However, there is a limit to the amount of money that can be paid to a family. If the total benefits payable to the retiree's spouse and children exceed this limit, their benefits will be reduced proportionately. Nevertheless, the retiree's benefit will not be affected.

As further discussed below, eligible family members may include: (i) a spouse age 62 or older; (ii) a spouse under age 62 if he or she is taking care of the retiree's child who is under age 16 or disabled; (iii) a former spouse; (iv) children up to age 18; (v) children age 18-19 if they are full-time elementary or secondary students; and (vi) children over age 18 if they are disabled.

Spousal Benefit

A spouse is entitled to Social Security benefits even if he or she never worked. If the married couple is over age 65 when the retiree's benefits begin, the spouse may be entitled to receive an additional amount equal to 50 percent of the retiree's benefit. A spouse may begin collecting benefits prior to age 65 provided the retiree is receiving benefits. However, if the spouse begins collecting benefits before age 65, his or her benefit is permanently reduced by a percentage based on the number of months before he or she reaches age 65.

For example, a spouse who begins collecting benefits at age 65 would receive approximately 46 percent of the retiree's full retirement benefit. If that spouse begins collecting at age 63, the benefit amount would be reduced to approximately 42 percent, etc. Nevertheless, if the retiree's spouse is taking care of a child who is under the age of 16 or disabled and receiving Social Security benefits, the spouse is entitled to full benefits regardless of age.

If both spouses worked and are eligible for their own social security benefits, the SSA always pays the individual benefit first. However, if the individual's benefit as a spouse is higher than their retirement benefit, he or she will get a combination of benefits equaling the higher spouse benefit.

For example, if a husband qualifies for his own retirement benefit of $250 and a wife's benefit of $400, at age 65, he will receive his own $250 retirement benefit plus $150 from the wife's benefit for a total of $400. However, if he decides to take his own retirement benefit before reaching full retirement age, both benefit amounts will be reduced.

A divorced spouse is also entitled to receive benefits on a former spouse's Social Security record if the marriage lasted at least 10 years. The divorced spouse must be age 62 or older and unmarried. If the spouse has been divorced at least two years, he or she can get benefits even if the worker is not yet retired. However, the worker must have enough credits to qualify for benefits and be age 62 or older. The amount of benefits a divorced spouse receives has no effect on the amount of benefits a current spouse may obtain.

Unmarried Children Benefit

When an individual retires, monthly Social Security payments may also be made to unmarried children under age 18, or age 19 if still in elementary or secondary school, or children age 18 or over who were severely disabled before age 22 and who continue to be disabled. Each eligible child generally receives up to one-half of the retiree's full benefit.

APPLYING FOR RETIREMENT BENEFITS

The SSA advises people to apply for retirement benefits 3 months before they want their benefits to begin. Even if an individual does not intend to retire, he or she should still sign up for Medicare 3 months before reaching age 65.

An application for social security retirement benefits can be made by calling the SSA or by visiting one of the offices. The SSA's toll-free telephone number is 1-800-772-1213. People who are deaf or hard of hearing may call the SSA's toll-free "TTY" number, 1-800-325-0778.

The following information and original or certified copies of listed documents will be needed to process the application:

1. The applicant's Social Security number;

2. The applicant's birth certificate;

3. The applicant's W-2 forms or self-employment tax return for the last year;

4. The applicant's military discharge papers if he or she had military service;

5. The applicant's spouse's birth certificate and Social Security number if the spouse is applying for benefits;

6. The applicant's children's birth certificates and Social Security numbers, if applying for children's benefits;

7. Proof of U.S. citizenship or lawful alien status if the applicant—or the applicant's spouse or child if applying for their benefits—was not born in the U.S.; and

8. The name of the applicant's bank and account number so the benefits can be directly deposited into the account.

RETIRING BEFORE FULL RETIREMENT AGE

If you wish, you may retire before full retirement age and receive Social Security retirement benefits at a rate which is reduced a small percentage for each month before you reach that age. However, the earliest age you can start collecting benefits is 62. Benefits are reduced five-ninths of one percent for each month you are retired before age 65, up to a maximum of 20 percent for people who retire the month they reach 62.

For example, if you sign up for Social Security at 62 years of age, you will receive approximately 80% of your full retirement benefit. At 64 years of age, you will receive 93-1/3% of your full retirement benefit.

It is important to note that your benefit is permanently reduced if you elect to start receiving it earlier than your full retirement age. The advantage to early retirement is that you begin to receive benefits before full retirement age and thus receive them for a longer period of time.

WORKING BEYOND RETIREMENT AGE

Some senior citizens continue to work full-time beyond full retirement age, and do not sign up for Social Security. Delaying retirement can increase your Social Security benefit by increasing your average earnings and will earn you a special credit from the Social Security program. This credit takes the form of a designated percentage added to the retiree's Social Security benefit depending on year of birth.

These increases are added in automatically from the time the individual reaches full retirement age until he or she starts receiving benefits, or until age 70. For example, an individual born in 1943 or later will receive an additional 8 percent per year to their benefit for each year of delayed retirement beyond full retirement age.

A table depicting the percentage of increase in social security benefits for each year of delayed retirement beyond full retirement age according to year of birth is set forth at Appendix 10.

Individuals who return to work after they start receiving benefits may be able to receive a higher benefit based on those earnings. This is because Social Security automatically recomputes the benefit amount after the additional earnings are credited to the individual's earnings record.

Nevertheless, some individuals who continue to work after retirement age, while also receiving benefits, may have their social security benefits reduced or eliminated depending on their earnings. Currently, this provision only affects people under the age of 70, and the reduction only applies to earned income.

In 1998, the earnings limit was $9,120 for people under age 65, and $14,500 for people age 65 through 69. An individual can still receive their entire social security benefit provided their earnings do not exceed the designated limit. As set forth below, if the earnings exceed the designated limit, some or all of the social security benefit may be withheld. For individuals under age 65, the SSA deducts $1.00 in benefits for each $2.00 earned above $9,120. For individuals age 65 through 69, the SSA will deduct $1.00 in benefits for each $3.00 earned above $14,500.

Individuals are required to report their earnings up to age 70. In the year a recipient reaches age 70, they are only responsible for reporting their earnings for the months before the month they reach age 70. A recipient does not have to report their earnings if they are 70 or older.

Social security retirement benefits are not affected by income you may earn as a result of investments or savings you have set aside to supplement your retirement income.

PROOF OF BENEFITS

Every year, the SSA sends recipients an SSA-1099 form showing how much they received in the past year. This form can be used as proof of the benefit amount. SSA also sends a notice when the benefit amount increases because of an annual cost of living raise.

EMPLOYMENT PENSION BENEFITS

If an individual receives a retirement pension from their employment, and also paid social security taxes, their retirement pension will not affect their Social Security benefit. However, pensions from work that is not covered by Social Security—such as federal civil service employment and some state or local government systems—may reduce the amount of one's Social Security benefit.

REPRESENTATIVE PAYEES

If a family member entitled to receive Social Security or SSI benefits is legally incompetent or otherwise mentally or physically incapable of managing his or her benefits, another individual may be designated by the SSA to receive that family member's social security benefits. The designated individual is known as a "Representative Payee."

Although a friend or custodial institution—e.g., a nursing home—can be designated as a representative payee, the SSA prefers to appoint relatives who are personally concerned for the beneficiary. The Social Security or SSI benefits are sent directly to the representative payee who must manage the funds for the personal care and well-being of the beneficiary, and pay the beneficiary's bills from the funds.

Any remaining funds do not belong to the representative payee, but must be saved for the benefit of the recipient. The representative payee is obligated to report certain changes in the beneficiary's circumstances that could affect their continuing eligibility to receive benefits.

The role of the Representative Payee is discussed in further detail in Chapter 10 of this almanac.

THE COST OF LIVING ALLOWANCE (COLA)

From 1940 until 1950 virtually no changes were made in the Social Security program. Payment amounts were fixed, and no major legislation was enacted. Because the program was still very new, and because it was financed by low levels of payroll taxation, the value of social security retirement benefits was very low.

In fact, until 1951, the average value of the welfare benefits received under the old-age assistance provisions of the Act were higher than the retirement benefits received under Social Security. More elderly Americans were receiving old-age assistance than were receiving Social Security.

To help relieve this problem, major amendments were enacted in 1950. These amendments increased benefits for existing beneficiaries for the first time and dramatically increased the value of the program to future beneficiaries. By February 1951, there were more Social Security retirees than welfare pensioners, and by August 1951, the average Social Security retirement benefit exceeded the average old-age assistance grant for the first time.

A second increase was legislated for September 1952. Together these two increases almost doubled the value of Social Security benefits for existing beneficiaries. From that point on, benefits were increased only when Congress enacted special legislation for that purpose.

The law was changed in 1972, effective 1975, to provide for annual cost-of-living allowances based on the annual increase in consumer prices. This cost of living allowance (COLA) is an automatic annual increase in social security benefits given to help offset the effects of inflation on fixed incomes. Beneficiaries no longer have to wait for a special enactment by Congress to receive a benefit increase.

For example, Social Security and SSI benefits increased 1.3 percent in 1999 as a result of the annual cost-of-living adjustment. The increase began with benefits that Social Security beneficiaries received for December 1998. Increased payments to SSI recipients began on December 31. For Social Security beneficiaries, the average monthly benefit amount for all retired workers rose from $770 to $780. The maximum federal SSI monthly payments to an individual rose from $494 to $500. For a couple, the maximum federal SSI payment rose from $741 to $751.

A table of social security cost of living allowance (COLA) increases (1950-2003) is set forth at Appendix 11.

CHAPTER 6:
SOCIAL SECURITY DISABILITY INSURANCE

IN GENERAL

The Social Security Amendments of 1954 initiated a disability insurance program which provided the public with additional coverage against economic insecurity. At first, the program merely involved a disability "freeze" of a worker's Social Security record during the years when he or she was unable to work due to the disability. While this measure offered no cash benefits, it did prevent such periods of disability from reducing or wiping out retirement and survivors benefits.

On August 1, 1956, the Social Security Act was amended to provide benefits to disabled workers aged 50-65 and disabled adult children.

In September 1960, President Eisenhower signed a law amending the disability rules to permit payment of benefits to disabled workers of any age and to their dependents.

By 1960, 559,000 people were receiving disability benefits, with an average benefit payment of approximately $80 per month.

Almost 90 percent of persons aged 21-64 who worked in covered employment in 2003 can count on monthly cash benefits if they suffer a severe and prolonged disability. As of 2003, approximately 7,595,452 disabled workers and their dependents were receiving benefits.

A table setting forth the number of disabled workers and their dependents receiving benefits (1970-2003) is set forth at Appendix 12.

ELIGIBILITY FOR SOCIAL SECURITY DISABILITY INSURANCE BENEFITS (SSDIB)

If a person has to stop working at any time before age 65 due to health reasons, he or she may be eligible for social security disability insurance benefits. A person is eligible for benefits if: (i) they meet the Social Security standard for disability; and (ii) they are deemed "insured" because they have worked the required number of quarters for a person their age and contributed to the Social Security system.

If the individual is deemed disabled, benefits may start as early as five months after he or she becomes disabled, and he or she may be entitled to retroactive benefits for up to one year, depending on how much time elapsed between the onset of the disability and application filing date.

APPLYING FOR SOCIAL SECURITY DISABILITY BENEFITS

An individual should apply for social security disability benefits as soon as they become disabled. Nevertheless, benefits will not begin until the sixth full month of disability. This waiting period begins with the first full month after the date the SSA decides the disability began.

An application for disability benefits can be made by calling the Social Security Administration at 1-800-772-1213. SSA representatives will make an appointment for the application to be taken over the telephone or at any local Social Security office. People who are deaf or hearing-impaired may call the SSA toll-free "TTY" number, 1-800-325-0778.

The claims process for disability benefits is generally longer than for other types of Social Security benefits—from 60 to 90 days. This is because it takes longer to obtain medical information and to assess the nature of the disability in terms of one's ability to work. The applicant is advised to expedite this process by providing the original or certified copy of certain documents and information when he or she applies, including:

1. The applicant's Social Security number;

2. The applicant's birth certificate or other evidence of date of birth;

3. The applicant's military discharge papers, if he or she was in the military service;

4. The applicant's spouse's birth certificate and Social Security number if he or she is applying for benefits;

5. The applicant's children's birth certificates and Social Security numbers if they are applying for benefits;

6. The applicant's checking or savings account information, so their benefits can be directly deposited;

7. The names, addresses, and phone numbers of doctors, hospitals, clinics, and institutions that treated the applicant and the dates of treatment;

8. The names of all medications the applicant is taking;

9. The applicant's medical records from his or her doctors, therapists, hospitals, clinics, and caseworkers;

10. The applicant's laboratory and test results;

11. A summary of where the applicant worked in the past 15 years and the kind of work he or she performed;

12. A copy of the applicant's W-2 Form (Wage and Tax Statement), or if the applicant is self-employed, his or her federal tax return for the past year;

13. The dates of any prior marriages if the applicant's spouse is applying.

DETERMINING DISABILITY

Qualifying disabilities are usually determined by a state agency that handles health issues—generally known as a disability determination service—which must find that the individual is suffering from a physical or mental impairment that meets SSA criteria. This would include a determination as to whether the disability prevents the individual from participating in "any substantial gainful activity." In addition, the disability must have lasted a full year, or be expected to last a full year, or be expected to result in the individual's death within a year.

Some of the factors that determine whether the applicant suffers from a qualifying disability include:

1. Present Employment—If the disabled applicant is working, and his or her earnings average more than $500 a month, he or she generally cannot be considered disabled.

2. Severity of Condition—The applicant's impairments must interfere with basic work-related activities for the claim to be considered.

3. Disabling Impairment—The SSA will check to see if the applicant's condition is on the SSA list of disabling impairments. This list contains impairments for each of the major body systems that are so severe they automatically mean the applicant is disabled. If the applicant's condition is not on the list, the SSA must decide if it is of equal severity to an impairment on the list. If it is, the claim will be approved. If it is not, a further determination must be made.

4. Ability to Perform Prior Work—If the applicant's condition is severe, but not of the same or equal severity as an impairment on the SSA list, then the SSA must determine if the impairment interferes with the applicant's ability to do the work he or she did in the last 15 years. If it does not interfere, the claim will be denied. If it does, the claim will be given further consideration.

5. Ability to Work—If the applicant cannot do the work he or she did in the last 15 years, the SSA then determines whether the applicant can do any other type of work. The SSA considers the applicant's age, education, past work experience, and transferable skills, and reviews the job demands of occupations as determined by the Department of Labor. If the applicant cannot do any other kind of work, the claim will be approved. If the applicant can perform other types of work, the claim will be denied.

In order to assist in this determination, the SSA requires the applicant to complete a disability report detailing: (i) the type and extent of the applicant's disability; (ii) the affect the disability has had on the applicant's ability to work; (iii) information about the applicant's employment; (iv) information about the applicant's medical records; and (v) information about the applicant's education and training.

MEDICAL AUTHORIZATION FORM—HIPAA COMPLIANT

In order to comply with the requirements of the Health Insurance Portability and Accountability Act of 1996 (HIPAA), the SSA has devised a new medical authorization form known as an Authorization to Disclose Information to the Social Security Administration (SSA Form 827). This form is used by the SSA to obtain medical and other information to determine whether a claimant is disabled.

A sample Authorization to Disclose Information to the Social Security Administration (SSA Form 827) is set forth at Appendix 13.

CHAPTER 7:
SURVIVORS BENEFITS

IN GENERAL

When an eligible individual dies, social security benefits are payable to certain family members. These benefits are called *survivors benefits*. Approximately 97 percent of persons aged 20-49 who worked in covered employment in 2003 have acquired survivorship protection for their children under age 18, and their surviving spouses caring for children under age 16. As of 2003, approximately 6,809,688 survivors were receiving benefits.

A table setting forth the number of survivors receiving benefits (1970-2003) is set forth at Appendix 14.

To be eligible, the decedent must have worked during their life, paid social security taxes, and earned enough credits. The number of credits needed to be deemed eligible for survivors benefits depends on the age of the decedent. The younger the person is when they die, the fewer credits needed for family members to be eligible for survivors benefits.

Under a special rule, benefits can be paid to a surviving spouse and minor children even if the decedent does not have the number of credits needed. Under this rule, they may be eligible for benefits if the decedent had credit for one and one-half years of work in the three years prior to their death. In general, individuals earn a maximum of four credits per year, and forty credits are the maximum number needed to be eligible for all Social Security benefits.

ELIGIBLE FAMILY MEMBERS

Eligible family members generally include the surviving spouse, children and dependent parents.

Surviving Spouse

A surviving spouse is eligible for full benefits at age 65 or older, or reduced benefits as early as age 60. If the surviving spouse is disabled, benefits may begin as early as age 50. However, the surviving spouse's benefits may be reduced if he or she also receives a pension from a job where Social Security taxes were not withheld.

A surviving spouse is eligible at any age if he or she cares for the decedent's child who is under 16 or disabled and receiving benefits on the decedent's Social Security record.

In addition, a surviving divorced spouse may be eligible for benefits provided the marriage lasted 10 years or more, or if he or she is caring for the decedent's child who is under 16 or disabled and receiving benefits on the decedent's Social Security record. However, the child must be the surviving divorced spouse's natural or legally adopted child. Benefits paid to a surviving divorced spouse who is age 60 or older, or age 50 to 60 if disabled, will not affect the benefit rates for other survivors who are receiving benefits.

When a surviving spouse who is receiving benefits remarries, the remarriage has no effect on the benefits being paid to the decedent's minor children. In addition, if the new spouse wishes to adopt children already entitled to survivor's benefits, the adoption does not terminate a child's benefits. However, if the surviving spouse is receiving benefits solely because he or she is caring for the decedent's minor children, those benefits would end at the time of remarriage unless the surviving spouse is age 60, or age 50 and disabled. If the surviving spouse marries someone who is also receiving Social Security benefits, he or she may get benefits on the new spouse's record at age 62 or older if those benefits are higher.

Unmarried Children

Unmarried children are eligible if they are either under the age of 18, or up to age 19 if they are attending elementary or secondary school full-time. A child can get benefits at any age if he or she was disabled before age 22 and remains disabled. Under certain circumstances, benefits may also be paid to stepchildren, grandchildren or adopted children.

Dependent Parents

Dependent parents are eligible for benefits at age 62 or older.

APPLYING FOR SURVIVORS BENEFITS

It is important to apply for survivors benefits promptly because benefits are generally retroactive only up to 6 months. Application may be made by telephone or at any Social Security office. The following information and original or certified copies of listed documents will be needed to process the application:

1. The decedent's social security number;

2. The applicant's social security number;

3. A marriage certificate if the applicant is a surviving spouse;

4. The divorce papers if the applicant is a surviving divorced spouse;

5. Dependent children's social security numbers;

6. The decedent's W-2 forms or federal self-employment tax return for the most recent year; and

7. The name of the applicant's bank and account number for direct deposit of benefits into the account.

However, if the surviving spouse has already been getting spousal benefits on the decedent's social security record when he or she dies, the surviving spouse need only report the death to the SSA and their existing benefits will be redesignated as survivors benefits.

If the spouse is already receiving benefits on his or her own social security record, he or she needs to apply for survivors benefits to see whether they are entitled to more benefits as a surviving spouse.

Benefits being received by children will automatically be redesignated as survivors benefits once the death is reported to the SSA.

AMOUNT OF BENEFITS

The amount of survivors benefits one's family members receive from Social Security depends on the decedent's average lifetime earnings. Of course, the higher the earnings, the higher the benefit amount. The amount is calculated as a percentage of the decedent's basic Social Security benefit. In general, the following percentages apply:

1. Surviving spouse age 65 or older—100 percent.

2. Surviving spouse age 60-64—Approximately 71 to 94 percent.

3. Surviving spouse, any age, with a child under age 16—75 percent.

4. Children—75 percent.

The amount of benefits may be reduced if the recipient's earnings exceed certain limits. However, those earnings would reduce only the working individual's survivors benefits and not the benefits of other family members.

Family Maximum

Each family member entitled to a monthly benefit will receive one. The total benefits received by the family, however, cannot exceed the family maximum amount. The limit varies, but is generally equal to approximately 150 to 180 percent of the decedent's benefit rate. That amount is divided among all entitled dependents. The more dependents who receive benefits on the worker's Social Security record, the lower the benefit amount will be for each dependent.

Special One-Time Payment

There is a special one-time payment—currently $255—that can be paid to a surviving spouse or minor child provided they meet certain requirements and the decedent had enough work credits at the time of death.

CHAPTER 8:
SUPPLEMENTAL SECURITY INCOME (SSI)

IN GENERAL

In the 1970s, the Social Security Administration (SSA) became responsible for a new program known as Supplemental Security Income (SSI). The original Act of 1935 included programs for needy aged and blind individuals and, in 1950, needy disabled individuals were added. However, these three programs were known as the "adult categories" and were administered by state and local governments with partial Federal funding. Over the years, the state programs became more complex and payments were inconsistent among the states. For example, payments varied more than 300% from state to state.

In 1969, President Nixon identified a need to reform these programs and, in 1971, the Secretary of Health, Education and Welfare proposed that the SSA assume responsibility for the "adult categories." In the 1972 Social Security Amendment, Congress federalized the "adult categories" by creating the SSI program and assigned responsibility for its administration to the SSA. The SSA was chosen to administer the new program because of its reputation for successful administration of the existing social insurance programs.

SSI is basically a federal welfare program for adults and children who are disabled or blind, and people aged 65 and over with low income and few financial resources. General tax revenues from the U.S. Treasury are used to finance the SSI program.

A table setting forth the number of SSI beneficiaries and amount of payments distributed (1974-1997) is set forth at Appendix 15; and a table setting forth the number of recipients and payments made, according to age category (April 2004) is set forth at Appendix 16.

ELIGIBILITY

In order to be eligible for SSI payments, one's income and assets must fall below certain established limits. Not all assets are taken into account. For example, a home and personal belongings are not counted, but bank accounts and cash on hand are included in the calculation. In addition, although eligibility for SSI would not be affected by the ability of one's children to support them, any support actually received from one's children would be considered income for SSI purposes and could affect the amount of the payment.

Although SSI is a federal program, some states supplement the national payments and have established higher SSI rates and allow higher income limits than others. It is important, therefore, to ascertain your individual state's eligibility for the SSI program. Unlike the income limits, however, the SSI asset limits do not vary among the states.

You don't have to qualify for Social Security benefits in order to get SSI, and it is possible to get both Social Security and SSI. However, if you're applying based on a disability, you must meet the same standard for disability as with regular Social Security benefits.

BENEFITS

The SSI program provides a basic payment for an eligible individual and a larger amount for an eligible couple. The payment for a couple is lower than that made to two individuals because married people living together generally share expenses and live more economically than two people living independently.

People who qualify for SSI receive a check each month. The amount of benefit may vary depending on the recipient's state of residence and level of income. If you qualify for SSI, you are also automatically entitled to health care coverage under the Medicaid program. In addition, an SSI recipient may also be eligible for food stamps and other social services.

One can apply for SSI and Medicaid by completing forms provided by their local welfare office, department of social services or SSA office. If the application is approved, the recipient will be paid benefits based on the date the application was filed.

The SSA reviews every SSI case from time to time to make sure the individuals who are receiving checks are still eligible and entitled to receive benefits. The review also determines if the individuals are receiving the correct amounts.

RIGHT TO APPEAL AND REPRESENTATION

If the application for SSI benefits is not approved, the individual can appeal that decision. The procedure for appealing an SSI determination is similar to appealing for more Social Security benefits. An applicant has 60 days to submit a written request for reconsideration. The request should be sent to the local Social Security district office, and should state the reasons why he or she disagrees with the determination. Depending on the nature of the issue, either a case review, a formal conference or a hearing may follow.

If the applicant does not appeal the determination within 60 days, their options are limited unless they can show there was a good reason for filing late. Without such a showing, the applicant may be able to file a new application and seek retroactive collection of benefits, or try to reopen the claim by filing a petition with a judge who is specially designated to hear Social Security appeals.

As further discussed in Chapter 11 of this almanac, the applicant also has the right to designate a representative to act on his or her behalf in dealing with the SSA by filing an Appointment of Representative form (SSA Form 1696). Once an appointment of representative is filed with the SSA, the SSA will deal directly with that individual on all matters affecting the applicant's Social Security claim.

STATISTICS

In 1998, fifty-five percent of SSI recipients were between the ages of 18 and 64; 31 percent were aged 65 or older; and 14 percent were under age 18.

Federally-administered payments in November 1998 totaled nearly $2.6 billion; over $2.3 billion in Federal SSI payments, and $264 million in State supplementation.

The average monthly federally-administered payment in November 1998 was $359—including $447 to recipients under age 18, $384 to those ages 18 to 64, and $281 to persons aged 65 or older.

Over 2.4 million SSI recipients (37 percent) also received Social Security benefits, including 61 percent of those aged 65 or older, and 26 percent of those under age 65.

The total number of persons receiving Social Security benefits, SSI, or both in November 1998 was 48,391,444.

WELFARE REFORM RESTRICTIONS

The welfare reform movement brought about significant changes in the SSI program. The passage of the Contract with America Advancement Act of 1996 narrowed the number of people allowed to receive SSI disability benefits by requiring that drug addiction or alcoholism not be a material factor in their disability.

THE FOOD STAMP PROGRAM

In General

In 1964, Congress passed the Food Stamp Act, which established the most significant federally funded food plan in the United States. The mission of the Food Stamp Program is to end hunger and improve the nutrition and health of low income adults and children. The program is in operation in the 50 States, the District of Columbia, Guam and the U.S. Virgin Islands.

Individuals who work for low wages, are unemployed or work part-time, receive public assistance, are elderly or disabled and have a small income, or are homeless may be eligible for food stamps. The federal government pays for the amount of the benefit received. State public assistance agencies are responsible for administering the program, and fund the costs of determining eligibility and distributing the food stamps.

Food stamps can only be used for food items and for plants and seeds used to grow food. Food stamps cannot be used to purchase nonfood items. In most states today, food stamp benefits are delivered electronically to Electronic Benefits Transfer (EBT) accounts. Under this system, the recipient receives a plastic card with a magnetic strip, similar to a credit or debit card, to access their food stamp EBT account at authorized food retail outlets.

Applicants who are also applying for or receiving Supplemental Security Income (SSI) benefits may apply for food stamps at their local Social Security Administration office.

Eligibility

Under the food stamp eligibility rules, the applicant's assets and resources, such as bank accounts, cash, real estate, personal property, vehicles, etc., are considered in determining whether a household is eligible to get food stamps. Some resources are counted toward the allowable limit and some are not.

All households may have up to $2,000 worth of countable resources and still be eligible. Households may have up to $3,000 and still be eligible if at least one member is age 60 or older. The resources of people who are receiving SSI payments are not counted toward the limit.

Some assets and resources that will not be counted are the applicant's: (i) home and surrounding lot; (ii) household goods and personal belongings; and (iii) life insurance policies. In addition, if a vehicle is needed to transport a physically disabled household member, its value is not counted.

Examples of resources that will be counted are the applicant's: (i) cash and funds in checking and savings accounts; (ii) stocks and bonds; and (iii) land and buildings, other than the applicant's home and lot, that do not produce income.

In order to be eligible for food stamps, most households have to meet both a monthly gross income test and a monthly net income test to be eligible for food stamps. However, households in which all members are receiving SSI payments are considered to be eligible based on income, and households with one or more elderly members only have to meet the net income test, which is gross income minus certain deductions.

The Personal Responsibility and Work Opportunity Reconciliation Act of 1996 (PRWORA) virtually eliminated food stamp benefits to legal immigrants. However, on May 13, 2002, President Bush signed the "Farm Security and Rural Investment Act of 2002" which allows legal immigrants who meet the program's requirements, and who receive disability benefits, such as SSI, to qualify for the Food Stamp Program.

Special Rules for the Elderly and Disabled

For purposes of the Food Stamp Program, a person is considered elderly if he or she is 60 years of age or older. A person is considered disabled if he or she:

1. Receives Federal disability or blindness payments under the Social Security Act, including Supplemental Security Income (SSI) or Social Security disability or blindness payments;

2. Receives State disability or blindness payments based on SSI rules;

3. Receives a disability retirement benefit from a governmental agency because of a disability considered permanent under the Social Security Act;

4. Receives an annuity under the Railroad Retirement Act and is eligible for Medicare or is considered to be disabled based on the SSI rules;

5. Is a veteran who is totally disabled, permanently housebound, or in need of regular aid and attendance; or

6. Is a surviving spouse or child of a veteran who is receiving VA benefits and is considered to be permanently disabled.

Although a household is generally considered to include everyone who lives together and purchases and prepares meals together, if a person is 60 years of age or older and he or she is unable to purchase and prepare meals separately because of a permanent disability, the person and the person's spouse may be a separate household, for the purposes of food stamp eligibility, if the others they live with do not have very much income.

In addition, people are not normally eligible for food stamps if they receive their meals in an institutional setting. However, an exception exists for elderly and disabled persons, as follows:

1. Residents of federally subsidized housing for the elderly may be eligible for food stamps, even though they receive their meals at the facility.

2. Disabled persons who live in certain nonprofit group living arrangements may be eligible for food stamps, even though the group home prepares their meals for them.

More detailed information on the Food Stamp Program may be found in this author's legal almanac entitled Welfare Law, published by Oceana Publishing Company, Dobbs Ferry, New York.

CHAPTER 9:
MEDICARE AND SUPPLEMENTAL HEALTH CARE COVERAGE

IN GENERAL

Medicare is a federal health insurance program administered by the Social Security Administration (SSA), designated for seniors and people with disabilities, regardless of income. Medicare was passed into law on July 30, 1965 but beneficiaries were first able to enroll in the program on July 1, 1966. Medicare is an entitlement program funded by payroll taxes. The Medicare program is administered by private health insurance companies who contract with the federal government to process claims.

ELIGIBILITY AND COVERAGE

When a person reaches age 65, he or she usually becomes eligible for Medicare. Unfortunately, Medicare does not cover all health-related expenses, and it is wise to supplement Medicare with additional health insurance coverage.

For example, Medicare does not pay for dentures and routine dental care, eyeglasses, hearing aids, prescription drugs, routine physical checkups, orthopedic devices, and non-skilled nursing home care—items that account for a considerable portion of medical expenses, particularly for senior citizens.

As set forth below, there are two parts to the Medicare policy: (i) Part A Hospitalization Coverage; and (ii) Part B Medical Coverage.

Part A Hospitalization Coverage

Part A is hospital insurance that covers hospital care as well as skilled nursing facility, hospice and home health care. Under Part A, there is a designated deductible—i.e., an initial amount one must pay for their hospitalization before Medicare begins to pay any additional expenses. This amount—known as the hospital deductible—increases every January 1st.

Medicare Part A benefits are free to most people 65 and older. In general, anyone eligible for Social Security or Railroad Retirement Benefits are also eligible for free Part A benefits. Persons who have been receiving Social Security disability benefits for a period of 24 months also qualify for Part A hospital coverage. Others may be eligible for Medicare if they pay a monthly premium.

If an individual has enrolled in Medicare and is also working and covered under their employer's group health plan, Medicare is still the primary payer if the employer has less than 20 employees. Medicare is the secondary payer if the employer has 20 or more employees and provides group health insurance. However, because Medicare Part A is free, an eligible individual should sign up for Part A once they are eligible, whether or not they have other insurance.

Eligible persons receive a health insurance card, known as a Medicare card, to claim their benefits. Persons already receiving Social Security automatically receive Medicare cards as part of their Social Security benefits.

Under Part A, the duration of care per benefit period is limited. A *benefit period* begins when the patient first enters a hospital or other facility, and ends after he or she has been discharged from the facility for a continuous period of at least 60 days from the date of discharge. This rule is simply a measurement device. There is no limit to the number of periods in which one may receive benefits. The benefit periods depend on the type of care received, as follows:

Hospital Care

Part A entitles the patient to 90 days of in-hospital care for each *benefit period*. There is a deductible for each benefit period. In addition, the patient has to pay a *co-insurance amount* for days 61 through 90. After the patient has exhausted their 90 days of coverage, Medicare will pay for an additional 60 days of care during the patient's lifetime. The patient will have to pay a portion during these "reserve" days. Additional coverage may be obtained through the purchase of a MediGap policy, which is further discussed below.

Hospitals cannot refuse patients on the ground that their health coverage is through Part A of Medicare. Remember, though, not all hospital stays or services are covered by Medicare. It is the hospital's responsibility to inform you if something is not covered.

Skilled Nursing Facility Benefits

Part A entitles the patient to 100 days of care in a Medicare-certified skilled nursing facility (SNF) per benefit period, provided: (i) the patient was hospitalized for at least three days during the 30 days prior to admission in the SNF and (ii) the patient needs and receives daily skilled services. Medicare defines "daily" as seven days a week of skilled nursing and five days a week of skilled therapy. Skilled nursing and therapy services include evaluation and management as well as observation and assessment of a patient's condition. Medicare pays for the first 20 days in full. For days 21 through 100, the patient pays a portion of the costs.

Home Health Care Benefits

Medicare Part A covers up to 35 hours a week of home health aide and *skilled nursing services* if a patient is homebound and requires skilled services on an *intermittent* basis. *Skilled nursing services* include the administration of medication, tube feedings, catheter changes and wound care. *Intermittent* usually means less than five days per week, but some people who receive home health care services up to seven days a week will be covered if the services are only needed for a finite and predictable amount of time. A patient can also qualify for up to 35 hours per week of home health aide services if they are homebound and need skilled physical, speech or occupational therapy.

To be covered, the patient must receive services from a Medicare-certified Home Health Agency (CHHA). Medicare home health coverage is available indefinitely so long as the patient remains homebound and continues to require skilled nursing services on an intermittent basis or skilled therapy services.

There is no prior hospitalization requirement and the benefit covers individuals with chronic illnesses as well as those who are acutely ill. The benefit is available at no cost to the patient, and there is no deductible or co-insurance required.

Hospice Benefits

Under Part A, hospice benefits are available to terminally ill patients. Medicare will cover 95 percent of the cost of hospice care, and the patient will have to pay the remaining five percent. Once the patient elects Medicare hospice benefits, he or she becomes ineligible to receive benefits for hospital care related to the terminal illness.

Part B Medical Coverage

Part B of the medicare policy covers most reasonable and necessary health-related expenses, other than hospitalization, including certain physician services, therapy services, outpatient hospital care, laboratory and diagnostic tests, supplies, durable medical equipment such as a wheelchair, and many other specified medical expenses not covered by Part A. Medicare sets approved charges for all of the medical services it covers.

Medicare does not cover many common health expenses, such as prescription drugs, routine checkups, vision and hearing care, custodial care, or dental care. It also does not cover experimental procedures.

In 1997, Congress passed a law which set forth new covered preventive care services at no extra cost, including: (i) yearly mammograms; (ii) pap smears including pelvic and breast examinations; (iii) colorectal cancer screening; (iv) bone mass measurement; (v) flu and pneumonia shots; and (vi) diabetes glucose monitoring and diabetes education for individuals with diabetes.

Anyone who is eligible for Part A hospital coverage is eligible for Part B medical coverage, however, Part B is not free. There is a monthly premium that increases every January 1st.

Part B medical coverage, unlike Part A, is based on a calendar year, rather than on benefit periods. The Part B medical coverage yearly deductible is $100.00 dollars. After the deductible is paid, Medicare pays 80% percent of the approved reasonable charges for covered services for the balance of the year.

Unfortunately, many health care providers charge substantially more than Medicare's approved charge for their services, and the patient must pay for any charges that are above the approved Medicare rate. For example, there is no limit on what ambulance companies and durable medical equipment suppliers may charge. The Medicare-approved portion may represent only a small part of the total bill.

Some health care providers, however, "take assignment," which means that they agree to accept Medicare's approved charge as payment in full. Medicare pays 80% of the approved charge, and the patient pays the remaining twenty percent. The local Medicare carrier has a directory that lists all doctors and suppliers in a particular area who always take assignment. To limit the amount one pays for medical expenses, it is a good idea to obtain a copy of this directory and use it when choosing health care providers.

When doctors don't "take assignment," federal law limits the amount that they may charge Medicare patients to 15% above Medicare's approved charge. Some states, including Massachusetts, Minnesota, Rhode Island, Pennsylvania, Ohio, Connecticut, Vermont and New York, have even stricter limits.

If an individual waits to enroll in Part B until he or she is older than 65, their monthly premium may be higher, since Medicare imposes a ten percent premium penalty for every year enrollment is delayed. However, if an individual is working and covered under their employer's group health plan, they may delay enrolling without a penalty until seven months after retirement.

However, it may not be cost-effective to sign up for Part B if you are already covered under an employer group health plan. That's because you will have to pay Medicare's Part B monthly premium and annual deductible, and your returns will be limited. In addition, it may be wise to stay in your employer's health plan after retirement, if that is an option, since any new insurance plans, including Medigap, may exclude pre-existing health problems for up to six months.

DENIAL OF MEDICARE CLAIMS

Under Medicare Part A hospital coverage, if a Medicare claim is denied, the hospital or Medicare review board must inform the claimant in writing if their stay will not—or will no longer—be covered by Medicare. The denial notice will set forth the procedures to follow in order to have the denial reconsidered. Many such denials are overturned.

If, after reconsideration, the claimant is still not satisfied, there are further remedies for appealing the decision. A large number of appeals are successful.

Under Medicare Part B coverage, if a claim is denied, the claimant will receive an "Explanation of Medicare Benefits." The claimant then has six months to ask for the denial to be reconsidered and overturned. If the claim is again rejected, the claimant has an additional six months to request a hearing through their local Medicare carrier. If the claim is again denied, the claimant has 60 days to request a hearing before an administrative law judge.

MEDICARE + CHOICE

In 1997, Congress passed a law which made many changes in the Medicare program, including a new section known as *Medicare + Choice*, which creates new health plan options for Medicare recipients.

Under the new law, a Medicare recipient can decide to: (i) continue receiving Medicare benefits under the original Medicare plan, (ii) continue receiving Medicare benefits under the original Medicare plan supplemented by one of ten available Medigap insurance policies, as further discussed below; or (iii) change to a plan that gives them at least the same, and possibly more, benefits than under the original Medicare plan.

There are differences among the new health plans including: (i) the cost; (ii) the availability of extra benefits; and (iii) the participant's choice in using certain doctors, hospitals and other medical providers.

In order to be eligible for Medicare + Choice, a recipient must have Medicare Parts A and B, and not have permanent kidney failure. Nevertheless, no matter which health plan option one chooses, they are still in the Medicare program and are still entitled to all of the services Medicare covers.

A Medicare Patient's Statement of Rights is set forth at Appendix 17.

Additional health care options available under the Medicare + Choice program include:

Medicare Managed Care Plan

A Medicare managed care plan is a Medicare approved network of doctors, hospitals, and other health care providers that agrees to give care in return for a set monthly payment from Medicare. Some managed care plans may provide extra benefits, and some may charge the participant a premium.

A managed care plan may be any of the following: (i) A Health Maintenance Organization (HMO); (ii) Provider Sponsored Organization (PSO); Preferred Provider Organization (PPO); or a Health Maintenance Organization with a Point of Service Option (POS).

An HMO or PSO usually asks the participant to use only the doctors and hospitals in the plan's network. If so, there are little or no out-of-pocket cost for covered services. A PPO or POS usually lets the participant use doctors and hospitals outside of the plan for an extra out-of-pocket cost.

Private Fee-for-Service Plan (PFFS)

A private fee-for-service plan (PFFS) is a Medicare-approved private insurance plan. Medicare pays the plan a premium for Medicare-covered services. A PFFS Plan provides all Medicare benefits. A PFFS Plan is not the same as a Medigap policy.

The PFFS Plan, rather than Medicare, decides how much to pay for the covered services the participant receives. Providers may bill the participant more than the plan pays, up to a limit, and the participant must pay the difference. It is likely that the participant will pay a premium for a PFFS plan.

Medicare Medical Savings Account Plan (MSA)

A Medicare medical savings account plan (MSA) is a health insurance policy with a high yearly deductible. This is a test program for up to 390,000 Medicare beneficiaries. Medicare pays the premium for the Medicare MSA Plan and deposits money into a separate Medicare MSA established by the participant. The participant uses the money in the Medicare MSA to pay for medical expenses.

The participant can accumulate money in their Medicare MSA to pay for extra medical costs. The insurance policy has a high deductible and there are no limits on what providers can charge above what is paid by the Medicare MSA Plan. A participant can only enroll in a Medicare MSA Plan during the month of November, and must remain in the plan for a full year.

Further information about the Medicare + Choice program may be obtained from the State Health Insurance Assistance Program in an individual's area. The State Health Insurance Assistance Program will help an individual with Medicare questions or provide information about other available health care options.

A directory of State Health Insurance Assistance Programs is set forth at Appendix 18.

SUPPLEMENTAL HEALTH INSURANCE PROGRAMS

Medigap Insurance

Medicare does not pay for all of an individual's medical expenses. Therefore, eligible Medicare recipients may also purchase supplemental coverage known as Medigap insurance. Medigap policies generally pay for medical-related expenses not reimbursed by Medicare, such as hospital deductibles and co-payments.

Medigap policies are designed to supplement Medicare and generally do not cover long-term care, although some policies do provide for skilled nursing home care and at-home recovery care. There are ten variations of Medigap plans available through private insurance companies. The basic benefits offered under all plans include:

1. Hospital co-insurance;

2. Full coverage for 365 additional hospital days to be used after exhaustion of Medicare hospital reserve days;

3. Twenty percent co-payment for physician and other Part B services; and

4. Three pints of blood.

There are a number of additional benefits available depending upon the plan you select. These benefits include:

1. Coverage of the Medicare hospital deductible;

2. Skilled nursing facility daily co-insurance;

3. Coverage of the Part B $100 deductible;

4. Eighty percent of emergency medical costs outside the U.S. during the first two months of a trip;

5. Payment to cover the difference when a doctor's fees are over the Medicare-approved charge;

6. At-home custodial care in addition to and in conjunction with Medicare-approved home care;

7. Some prescription drug coverage; and

8. Some preventive medical care coverage.

There are many services a Medigap plan will not cover. These include:

1. Custodial care—such as feeding, bathing and grooming—either at home or in a nursing home;

2. Long-term skilled care in a nursing home;

3. Unlimited prescription drugs;

4. Vision care;

5. Dental care; or

6. Private nurses.

In addition, if Medicare refuses to cover medical care because it is unreasonable and unnecessary or experimental, Medigap will not cover it either.

Once you select a Medigap policy, you have 30 days to review the plan and cancel it without penalty. You also are allowed to change or cancel your policy once a year, although in most states your insurer can reject your application for more comprehensive coverage. However, if you wish to downgrade your policy, you may do so.

If an individual does opt to enroll in a Medigap plan, it's usually best to do so during the six months following enrollment in Medicare Part B. During that period, insurance companies must let the insured sign up for the plan of their choice, without regard to health or age.

Further information concerning Medigap insurance policies may be obtained from the National Insurance Consumer Helpline at (800) 942-4242.

The Qualified Medicare Beneficiary Program

Persons who receive Medicare and have income and resources below a certain amount may be eligible for the Qualified Medicare Beneficiary (QMB) program. Under the QMB program, the State pays Medicare premiums, deductibles and coinsurance for persons who qualify for the program

Medicaid

Medicaid is a government program designed to provide health services, including nursing home care, to persons who are financially eligible. Medicaid eligibility is determined by a number of factors, the most important of which is income level.

Only certain classes of individuals are eligible for Medicaid, including: (i) elderly persons who, although eligible for Medicare, cannot afford it; (ii) disabled persons; (iii) pregnant women; and (iv) children from low-income households.

Each state formulates and administers its own Medicaid program, following federal government guidelines, through matching federal funds based on the state's per capita income. Within these guidelines, states have considerable freedom in managing their own Medicaid program, thus coverage varies from state-to-state. For example, individual states set the financial eligibility criteria for Medicaid in their jurisdiction, often well below federally established poverty levels.

Medicaid offers more comprehensive coverage than Medicare. However, the program's low reimbursement levels discourages private medical providers from participating in the program.

Medicaid pays for costs not covered by Medicare for elderly persons who qualify for Medicare but cannot afford the Part A hospital deductible or Part B premium. Nevertheless, Medicaid is generally not an alternative resource to most persons in need of long-term care because of the stringent restrictions. To be eligible for Medicaid, one must first exhaust all of their assets and savings—not including their home—a process known as "spending down."

An exception exists under the spouse impoverishment provisions of Medicare, which provide that the spouse of a person receiving long-term care in a nursing home is permitted to keep a certain dollar amount of assets and income, and still be eligible for Medicaid. However, the amount one is allowed to retain is still very modest.

Older Americans Act

Under the *Older Americans Act of 1965*, states are allocated federal funds for the purpose of setting up agencies designed to provide services to persons over the age of 60. Unfortunately, these services are limited in scope, subject to eligibility standards, and not available in all areas. Services provided under this statute may include home health care, adult day care, homemaker services, transportation, and meal delivery programs.

Social Services Block Grants (Title XX)

The Social Services Block Grants program, established under Title XX of the Social Security Act provides for allocation of federal funds to the states to assist low-income persons with non-medical daily living services, such as those provided under the Older Americans Act. These services are also not widely available and thus may not be an option for most persons.

Anyone over 65 who is eligible for Social Security or Railroad Retirement Benefits—a program similar to Social Security for railroad employees, their spouses and survivors—is automatically eligible. People with disabilities who have received Social Security Disability Income for at least 24 months and some people who are receiving regular dialysis or have received a kidney transplant because of kidney failure are also automatically eligible. U. S. citizens are automatically eligible as are permanent legal residents who have been continuously residing in the United States for at least five years, though they must file an application.

LONG-TERM HEALTH CARE

This section discusses the availability of an insurance policy to protect individuals in need of care over an extended period of time. Unlike acute care—short-term, recuperative care provided by a hospital—long-term care is the type of care given to persons who have become disabled or who suffer from a chronic illness.

Long-term care is often a concern for senior citizens. Although many senior citizens are able to live out their lives independently and in good health, many others have health care problems which render them infirm and dependent on others to help them with their daily activities.

In 1991, 7 million senior citizens were in need of long-term care. This number is expected to increase to almost 9 million by the year 2000. The majority of the cost of this care is borne by the patients and their families. This is particularly burdensome in the retirement years when most older persons are on fixed incomes.

Home care costs can range from $50 to $200 per day, depending on the level of care and the number of hours provided. The average cost of care in a nursing home is estimated at $25,000 per year and more, depending on the facility, the location, and the level of care provided. Nursing home care is rarely covered by private insurance. If a senior citizen doesn't qualify under the Medicare or Medicaid programs, he or she must finance their own care.

Nursing Homes

The term nursing home generally refers to a residential facility that provides shelter and care for senior citizens who are unable to live independently. Many elderly recipients of social security benefits reside in nursing home settings.

As set forth below, there are three types of nursing homes.

Personal Care Nursing Facility

Personal Care Nursing Facilities provide the senior citizen who does not need any special medical care with room and board and basic assistance with daily activities. Medicare and Medicaid generally does not pay for this type of long-term care.

Medicaid Nursing Facility

Medicaid Nursing Facilities provide the senior citizen with a limited range of skilled nursing care, rehabilitation services, and other necessary health-related care. Medicare does not pay for residence in such facilities, however Medicaid may reimburse the costs of such care provided a doctor certifies that the senior citizen is in need of this level of care. Further, the resident must meet certain financial guidelines to qualify for admission.

Medicare Skilled Nursing Facility (SNF)

Medicare Skilled Nursing Facilities provide the senior citizen with the most highly skilled nursing care available outside of a hospital setting, including many specialized services. Medicare pays up to 150 days per calendar year for residence at such a facility, provided your physician certifies that you are in need of such a high level of care.

Federal law guarantees nursing home residents certain rights, applicable whether it is a publicly or privately owned institution. These rights include, but are not limited to: (1) the right to be free from physical or mental harm or abuse; (2) the right to privacy; and (3) the right to choose your own physician and participate in your health care decisions.

Long-Term Health Care Insurance Policies

There are long-term care insurance policies available to individuals who want to plan ahead for the possibility of needing long-term care in the future. With the exception of the Medicaid program, which has limited eligibility, much of what is covered under long-term health care insurance is either not covered at all, or only partially covered under Medicare or private health insurance policies.

Responding to this need, a large number of insurance companies have stepped in to fill the gap, providing a variety of insurance policies covering long-term care. If one is considering purchasing such a policy, it would be prudent to review the benefits being offered by the various companies in order to choose the policy that best fits your needs.

Although long-term care insurance can be very helpful if it is ever needed, it can also be quite costly, ranging anywhere from $250 to over $2000 per year for the average senior citizen who is in good health. Before taking on this considerable expense, it would be wise to carefully assess one's individual situation and investigate all resources available from other programs. Some of the factors one should consider when assessing the need for long-term care insurance, include:

1. The individual's present financial situation and projected financial situation following retirement;

2. The individual's ability to afford long-term care insurance;

3. The programs the individual expects to be eligible for upon retirement and whether they will be able to meet his or her needs;

4. The likelihood that the individual will require long-term care in the future, based on his or her present health and family history; and

5. The alternative resources the individual expects to have if long-term care is needed, such as family and friends, and the availability of community-based services.

Since long-term care insurance is a fairly recent development, one must be very careful in selecting and evaluating the various policies available, and inquiring into the background and stability of the companies offering such insurance.

Every policy generally contains some restrictions and limitations, and some policies may not be available due to such factors as age and health. Carefully read all of the provisions of the policy before making your decision. If any of the provisions are unclear, seek professional assistance in understanding the policy. In general, the policy should be flexible enough to cover all levels of nursing home and home health care without undue restrictions, such as stipulations as to the facilities at which the individual can receive care. In addition, the policy should have a renewal guarantee.

Although the provisions, limitations and restrictions of long-term care insurance policies may vary, there are a number of typical provisions found in most policies. Some of these provisions are discussed below.

Coverage

Long-term care insurance policies typically cover nursing home care. Some policies cover all levels of nursing home care—skilled nursing care, intermediate care, and custodial care—while others may cover only a certain level of care, such as skilled nursing care. It is best to purchase a policy that covers all levels of nursing home care, since long-term skilled nursing care is not usually needed. It is more likely that a person will need a lesser level of nursing home care, such as custodial care, over an extended period of time. Also be aware of any limitations or prerequisites to such care.

Home health care is generally provided for in long-term care insurance policies. Again, however, one must be aware of any limitations on the availability of such care. For example, some policies may only provide home health care after hospitalization, which may not be necessary in every case even though the individual may be in need of home health care services. In addition, long-term care insurance may include coverage for such services as assistance with household chores, shopping, transportation and personal hygiene, as well as long-term skilled nursing care.

Benefits

Most policies pay only a preset daily benefit for nursing home care or home health care, and the difference between the amount covered by the insurance and the actual costs of care is borne by the insured. Some policies allow the insured to pay higher premiums in return for higher daily benefits. When considering inflation, one must be aware that in many cases the benefits payable under the policy will not be increased. Therefore, the individual will be responsible for any escalation in the costs of care due to inflation.

To avoid this problem, one must shop around for a policy that provides for benefit increases over time due to inflation. One must also be aware of any limits the policy places on the duration of care and the benefits payable under the policy. Generally, policies that provide for a longer duration of care and benefits will be more costly.

Policy Restrictions

Most long-term care policies contain various restrictions. For example, a restriction on preexisting conditions—conditions that existed prior to the policy's effective date—typically denies the insured any benefits connected with those specific health conditions for a designated waiting period after the effective date of the policy.

Another restriction that often appears in long-term care insurance policies is the waiting period, known as the elimination period, during which the policy does not pay benefits. For example, if a policy specifies that benefits for home health care will begin on the 21st day, that means the insured is responsible for payment out-of-pocket for the first 20 days of home health care. Lower cost policies may contain waiting periods that are considerably longer. In considering a policy's waiting periods, you must determine whether it is worth the higher premium to insure that you will receive benefits at the earliest possible date.

To obtain further information on all aspects of long-term care, one should contact their State Office of Aging or State Office of Long-Term Care Ombudsman. In addition, there are a number of national and state organizations and agencies which are dedicated to helping the elderly.

A directory of the State and National Offices of Aging is set forth at Appendix 19, and a directory of the National Organizations of the Elderly is set forth at Appendix 20.

CHAPTER 10:
REPRESENTATIVE PAYEES

IN GENERAL

In general, a person has the right to receive their own Social Security check and manage their own finances. However, in some circumstances, the Social Security Administration (SSA) may appoint a representative payee for the beneficiary. For example, if the SSA has reason to believe that the beneficiary may have spent their benefits in ways that were harmful to the beneficiary, or if the beneficiary has a physical or mental disability that would affect their ability to properly manage their benefits, another person may be appointed by the SSA to handle that person's Social Security matters.

The person who is appointed is known as a representative payee. Once appointed, the person's benefits are paid to the payee on the beneficiary's behalf. The payee is appointed to manage Social Security funds only. A payee has no legal authority to manage non-Social Security income or medical matters.

The law requires minor children and legally incompetent adults to have payees. In all other situations, adult beneficiaries are presumed to be capable of managing benefits. If there is evidence to the contrary, however, the SSA may appoint a representative payee. If the beneficiary doesn't agree that they need a payee, or if they want a different payee than the one appointed by the SSA, the beneficiary has 60 days to appeal the decision by sending a letter to the SSA.

INDIVIDUAL PAYEES

The representative payee may be a relative, friend or other interested party. The payee must submit proof of identity and show their social security card or Employer Identification Number (EIN). The payee must be a person who has never been shown to have misused anyone's Social Security benefits and must have never been found guilty of a crime committed against the SSA. In addition, the payee must attend an interview with the beneficiary at the local SSA office.

ORGANIZATIONAL PAYEES

Many beneficiaries do not have a family member or friend to serve as their representative payee. In an effort to ensure that beneficiaries who are unable to handle their own benefits have qualified payees to act in this capacity, the SSA looks to state, local and community sources to fill the need, and recruits organizations that already provide some case management services, spiritual guidance or community assistance, to provide this service.

Generally, organizations make good payees because they have plenty of experience with services and resources within the community, and are able to obtain discounts on goods and services because there is strength in numbers. An organizational payee has the same obligation as an individual payee in making sure that the beneficiary's needs are met and good records are maintained. Unlike the individual payee, an organizational payee is permitted to charge a fee for this service, as further discussed below.

RESPONSIBILITIES OF THE REPRESENTATIVE PAYEE

The representative payee has certain obligations to the beneficiary, as follows:

1. The payee is legally required to use the beneficiary's benefits in a proper manner. As further discussed below, the payee must determine the beneficiary's total needs and use the benefits received in the best interests of the beneficiary.

2. If the beneficiary does not live with the payee, he or she must keep apprised of the beneficiary's needs and conditions, e.g. by visiting the beneficiary and consulting with the beneficiary's custodians.

3. The payee must notify the SSA of any change in the payee's circumstances that would affect performance of their responsibilities.

4. The payee must report any event that will affect the amount of benefits the beneficiary receives, or the beneficiary's eligibility for benefits.

5. The payee must save any money left after meeting the beneficiary's current needs in an interest bearing account or savings bonds for the beneficiary's future needs.

6. The payee must keep records of all payments received and how they are spent and/or saved.

7. The payee must provide benefit information to social service agencies or medical facilities that serve the beneficiary.

8. The payee must help the beneficiary get medical treatment when necessary.

9. The payee must complete written reports accounting for the use of funds.

10. The payee must return any payments to which the beneficiary is not entitled to the SSA.

11. The payee for a child receiving SSI payments is required to obtain treatment for the child's disabling condition when treatment is determined to be medically necessary. If the payee is not sure whether treatment is required, he or she must contact the local SSA office. If the payee fails to obtain medical treatment for the child, the SSA may remove that person as the payee for the child.

PROHIBITED ACTIONS

Representative payees are required by law to use the benefits properly. If a payee misuses benefits, he or she must repay the misused funds to the beneficiary. A payee who is convicted of misusing funds may be fined and/or imprisoned. A representative payee may not:

1. Sign legal documents, other than Social Security documents, on behalf of a beneficiary.

2. Have legal authority over earned income, pensions, or any income from sources other than Social Security or SSI.

3. Use a beneficiary's money for the payee's personal expenses, or spend funds in a way that would leave the beneficiary without necessary items or services.

4. Put a beneficiary's Social Security or SSI funds in their account or in another person's account.

5. Use a child beneficiary's "dedicated account" funds for basic living expenses. However, this only applies to disabled/blind SSI beneficiaries under age 18.

6. Keep conserved funds once he or she no longer the payee.

7. Charge the beneficiary for services unless authorized by SSA to do so.

USE OF BENEFITS

The representative payee must apply the Social Security payments only for the beneficiary's use and benefit. First, the beneficiary's day-to-day needs must be met. This would include allocating funds for food and shelter. Benefits may then be used for the beneficiary's personal needs, such as clothing, recreation, and other expenses. Benefits can then be used to pay for medical and dental needs that are not covered by health insurance, Medicare or Medicaid, or provided by the beneficiary's residential institution, if applicable.

If there are funds left over once the beneficiary's basic needs are met, the payee may use the money to pay for items that could improve the beneficiary's life, such as school tuition or training programs. Otherwise, any remaining funds must be saved and/or invested in trust for the beneficiary. If the beneficiary is in a nursing home or other residential institution, benefits should be used to pay for the beneficiary's care, and a minimum amount of $30 per month should be set aside for the beneficiary's personal needs.

A beneficiary's funds can also be used as a down payment on a home owned wholly or partially by the beneficiary, and for the beneficiary's reasonable share of the monthly household expenses. Funds may also be used to renovate the home to make it safer and more accessible to the beneficiary, e.g., by installing a wheelchair ramp. Furniture may be purchased with a beneficiary's funds even if those items will be shared with other members of the household. In addition, the beneficiary's money can be used for the down payment and monthly payments on an automobile purchased for and owned by the beneficiary.

If the representative payee is uncertain about whether an expenditure of funds is proper, he or she may contact the local SSA office for guidance.

Special Situations

Beneficiaries Receiving SSI Benefits

An SSI beneficiary must not have resources worth more than $2,000 individually, or $3,000 for couples. Insofar as some purchases could make the beneficiary ineligible for payments, the representative payee should check with the local SSA office before making a major purchase for an SSI beneficiary.

Not all resources are counted, e.g., a house or car is excluded from the calculation. However, cash not spent is counted as a resource. Thus, if the beneficiary receives a retroactive payment of a large sum of money, any amount exceeding $2,000 must be spent within six months or an overpayment may occur and benefits may stop.

Blind or Disabled Children Receiving SSI Benefits

Certain large past-due SSI payments to blind or disabled children covering more than six months of benefits must be paid directly into a separate account in a financial institution, known as a "dedicated account." The dedicated account must be kept separately from any other savings or checking account set up for the beneficiary. Except for certain subsequent past-due payments, no other funds may be commingled into the account. Money in the dedicated account, as well as interest earned on that money, is not countable as an SSI resource.

Money in a dedicated account must be used only for the following allowable expenses for the benefit of the child:

1. Medical treatment and education or job skills training.

2. If related to the child's disability, personal needs assistance; special equipment; housing modification; and therapy or rehabilitation.

3. Any other item or service related to the child's disability that the SSA determines is appropriate, such as the cost of improving the home to accommodate the child's impairment, or legal fees incurred in establishing the child's claim for benefits.

If the representative payee knowingly uses money from a dedicated account for anything other than the expenses listed above, the payee must repay the SSA an amount equal to what the payee spent from the payee's own funds.

TYPE OF ACCOUNT

The SSA recommends that the representative payee have the beneficiary's monthly benefits directly deposited into a checking or savings account. The payee must not mix the beneficiary's funds with his or her own funds—a practice known as "commingling." To protect the beneficiary's funds, checking and savings accounts must show the beneficiary as the only owner. Neither the representative payee nor a third party can have ownership interest in the account. Any account title that, under state law, shows beneficiary ownership, and the representative payee as fiduciary, is acceptable. Nevertheless, while the beneficiary retains ownership interest, the account title should not permit the beneficiary to have direct access to the funds.

RECORDKEEPING

The representative payee is responsible for keeping records and reporting on the use of the beneficiary's benefits by completing a Representative Payee Report. The payee should keep these records for two years from the time the form is completed. The SSA will mail the appropriate form to the payee once a year.

INCOME TAX

Some people who receive Social Security benefits have to pay federal income tax on their benefits. At the beginning of each year, the SSA will mail the representative payee a Social Security Benefit Statement that shows the amount of benefits paid during the previous year. This statement should be given to the person who prepares the beneficiary's tax returns to use in determining whether any benefits are subject to tax.

ORGANIZATIONS THAT SERVE AS REPRESENTATIVE PAYEES

Sometimes nursing homes or other organizations that serve as representative payees place funds for several beneficiaries in a single checking or savings account. This is called a "collective account." This is usually acceptable, but special rules apply to these accounts, as follows:

1. The account title must show that the funds belong to the beneficiary and not the payee.

2. The account must be separate from the organization's operating account.

3. Any interest earned belongs to the beneficiary.

4. There must be clear and current records showing the amount of each beneficiary's share, and proper procedures for documenting credits and debits.

5. The account and supporting records must be made available, upon request, to the SSA.

Organizations serving as representative payees who are considering charging the beneficiary for past care and maintenance costs will need to get approval from the local SSA office. The SSA also needs to approve any decision to pool the personal funds of several beneficiaries to purchase an item that will benefit the group.

REPORTING CHANGES

The representative payee must advise the SSA if there are any changes that may affect the benefits received on behalf of the beneficiary. The payee is liable for repayment of any funds received if the payee failed to report any of the following events:

1. The beneficiary dies.

2. The beneficiary moves.

3. The beneficiary starts or stops working, no matter how small the amount of earnings.

4. A disabled beneficiary's condition improves.

5. The beneficiary starts receiving another government benefit, or the amount of the benefit changes.

6. The beneficiary will be outside the U.S. for 30 days or more.

7. The beneficiary is imprisoned for a crime that carries a sentence of over one month.

8. The beneficiary is committed to an institution by court order for a crime committed because of a mental impairment.

9. Custody of a child beneficiary changes or a child is adopted.

10. The beneficiary is a stepchild, and the parents divorce.

11. The beneficiary gets married.

12. The payee is no longer responsible for the beneficiary.

13. The beneficiary no longer needs a payee.

14. The payee is convicted of a felony.

15. The payee moves.

16. The beneficiary moves to or from a hospital, nursing home or other institution.

17. A married beneficiary separates from his or her spouse, or they begin living together again after a separation.

18. Someone moves into or out of the beneficiary's household.

19. The beneficiary has a change in income or resources.

20. Any changes in the family's income or resources that may affect a child's SSI benefit.

MEDICARE AND MEDICAID

A representative payee may need to help the beneficiary obtain medical services or treatment in which case the payee needs to show the Medicare card or State Medicaid Eligibility Card to the person or place providing the medical service. A record should be kept of medical services the beneficiary receives and medical expenses not covered by Medicare and Medicaid.

If the beneficiary has low income and few resources, the state may pay Medicare premiums and some out-of-pocket medical expenses. A person may qualify even if his or her income or resources are too high for SSI.

DEATH OF THE BENEFICIARY

If the beneficiary dies, saved benefits belong to his or her estate. They must be given to the legal representative of the estate or otherwise handled according to state law. When a person who receives Social Security benefits dies, no check is payable for the month of death, even if he or she dies on the last day of the month. Any check received for the month of death or later must be returned to the SSA. Nevertheless, an SSI check is payable for the month of death but the payee must return any SSI checks that are received after the month of death.

FEES

Individual representative payees cannot collect fees. A payee organization, however, may collect a fee from a Social Security or SSI beneficiary's monthly payment as reimbursement for expenses incurred in providing payee services to that beneficiary.

Before an organization can collect a fee for representative payee services, it must request authorization from the manager of the local SSA office. Once the organization is authorized, they are called a "Fees-for-Services" representative payee.

To collect a fee an organization must be:

1. A community based, nonprofit social service agency, which is bonded or licensed in the state in which it serves as payee, or

2. A state or local government agency with responsibility for income maintenance, social service, health care, or fiduciary responsibilities, and

3. Regularly serving as a representative payee for at least five beneficiaries, and is not a creditor of the beneficiary.

REIMBURSEMENT FOR EXPENSES

Some payee-related expenses can be reimbursed from the beneficiary's payment, such as out of pocket expenses incurred on behalf of the beneficiary. These expenses include:

1. The cost of postage to pay the beneficiary's bills;

2. The cost of money orders and/or new checks,

3. The cost of transporting the beneficiary to and from medical appointments;

4. Other reasonable items associated with performing the representative payee's duties.

Nevertheless, a "fees-for-services" organizational payee cannot collect reimbursement for these items because these items are considered "overhead" and are therefore covered by the fee.

APPEALING THE APPOINTMENT OF A REPRESENTATIVE PAYEE

The beneficiary has the right to appeal the decision that they need a representative payee, as well as the person or organization the SSA has chosen as the beneficiary's representative payee. The beneficiary has 60 days to appeal the decision by contacting the SSA, in writing.

If the beneficiary has a representative payee because of a physical or a mental disability, in order to become their own payee, the beneficiary must show the SSA that they are now mentally and physically able to handle their own Social Security benefits. In support of the appeal, the beneficiary may provide the SSA with the following documentation:

1. A doctor's statement that there has been a change in the beneficiary's condition and that the doctor believes they are able to care for themselves; or

2. An official copy of a court order saying that the court believes that the beneficiary can take care of themselves; or

3. Other evidence that shows the beneficiary's ability to take care of themselves.

The beneficiary is advised, however, that if the SSA believes the beneficiary's condition has improved to the point that they no longer need a representative payee, they may reevaluate the beneficiary's eligibility for Social Security benefits.

WITHDRAWING AS A REPRESENTATIVE PAYEE

If the representative payee decides to withdraw as payee for the beneficiary, he or she must notify the SSA immediately so that a new payee may be appointed as soon as possible. The payee must return any benefits, including interest and cash on hand, to the SSA. The funds will then be reissued to the beneficiary or to a new payee.

CHAPTER 11:
THE CLAIMANT'S RIGHT
TO REPRESENTATION

IN GENERAL

Dealing with the Social Security Administration (SSA) on social security matters can become complicated. Therefore, the applicant for Social Security benefits has the right to designate a representative to act on his or her behalf. Representatives are usually attorneys who are familiar with the Social Security system.

An applicant cannot designate someone who has been suspended or disqualified from representing others before the SSA or who may not, by law, act as a representative. The applicant can appoint one or more people in a firm, corporation or other organization as their representative, but may not appoint the firm, corporation or organization itself. The local SSA office has a list of organizations that can help an applicant find a representative.

At the hearing level, representatives are involved in approximately 80 percent of SSA cases. It is important to select an individual who is qualified to act in this capacity as he or she will have the authority to act on the applicant's behalf in most Social Security matters.

STANDARDS OF CONDUCT

All attorney and non-attorney representatives of claimants who practice before the Social Security Administration must comply with the Rules of Conduct and Standards of Responsibility for Representatives (Rules of Conduct) found at 20 C.F.R. §§ 404.1740 and 416.1540. The Rules of Conduct specify both affirmative obligations and prohibited conduct.

If a representative violates the Rules of Conduct, is not qualified to be either an attorney or non-attorney representative under 20 C.F.R. §§ 404.1705 and 416.1505, or has been convicted of a violation under section 206 of the Social Security Act, or otherwise acts improperly, the SSA may file charges and initiate proceedings to suspend or disqualify that representative from acting as a representative before the SSA. The representative may also face criminal prosecution.

Any person who believes that an attorney or non-attorney representative has acted in a manner that violates the Rules of Conduct should promptly report that representative to an SSA field or hearing office.

Improper acts include:

1. If the representative is or was an officer or employee of the United States, providing services as a representative in certain claims against, and other matters affecting, the Federal government.

2. Knowingly and willingly furnishing false information.

3. Charging or collecting an unauthorized fee or too much for services provided in any claim, including services before a court which made a favorable decision.

The SSA will not work with a representative who is suspended or disqualified from representing claimants.

DESIGNATING A REPRESENTATIVE

In order to designate a representative, the claimant must file an Appointment of Representative Form (SSA Form 1696) with the SSA. The representative must also accept the appointment by signing the form.

A sample Appointment of Representative Form (SSA Form 1696) is set forth at Appendix 21.

The SSA will continue to work with the designated representative until:

1. The claimant advises the SSA that the representative no longer represents them; or

2. The representative advises the SSA that he or she is withdrawing, or indicates that his or her services have ended, e.g. by filing a fee petition or by not pursuing an appeal.

Most legal services organizations will provide a lawyer free of charge to those unable to afford one.

A directory of National Legal Services for the Elderly is set forth at Appendix 22.

RESPONSIBILITIES OF THE REPRESENTATIVE

Once the Appointment of Representative form is filed with the SSA, the SSA will deal directly with that individual on all matters affecting the applicant's Social Security claim. A representative may:

1. Obtain information from the claimant's file;

2. Provide the SSA with evidence or information to support the claim;

3. Accompany the claimant, or attend on the claimant's behalf, any SSA interview, conference or hearing;

4. Request a reconsideration, hearing, or Appeals Council review on behalf of the claimant; and

5. Prepare the claimant and the claimant's witnesses for the SSA hearing.

The SSA will send the representative a copy of any decisions made on the claimant's claims, and the representative is expected to discuss the status of the claim with the claimant. Both the claimant and the representative are responsible for providing the SSA with accurate information. It is illegal to furnish false information knowingly and willfully.

FEES

A representative is entitled to request a fee for his or her services. As set forth below, certain services require fee approval while others do not.

Proceedings That Require SSA Fee Authorization

The SSA considers any claim or asserted right under Titles II, XVI, or XVIII of the Social Security Act, which results in the following, to be a proceeding before the SSA for fee authorization purposes:

1. An initial, revised, or reconsidered determination or action by a field office or processing center; or

2. A decision or action by an Administrative Law Judge or an Administrative Appeals Judge.

Proceedings that require SSA's fee authorization include, but are not limited to, services in connection with:

1. An application for Social Security monthly benefits, supplemental security income (SSI) payments, or a lump-sum death payment;

2. An application for hospital insurance benefits or supplemental medical insurance benefits;

3. A request to establish or continue a period of disability;

4. A request to modify the amount of benefits;

5. A request to reinstate benefits;

6. A request to waive recovery of an overpayment, or an appeal of an overpayment waiver denial determination; and

7. A request to revise an earnings record.

Situations When SSA Authorization Is Not Required

When all of the following conditions are present, the SSA does not need to authorize the representative's fee:

1. The claimant and affected auxiliary beneficiary are free of direct or indirect liability to pay a fee or expenses, either in whole or in part, to a representative or to someone else.

2. The entity which pays the fee and expenses incurred, if any, on behalf of the claimant or beneficiary is a nonprofit organization or a Federal, State, county, or city agency.

3. A government entity provides or administers the funds used to pay a fee or any expenses.

4. A representative submits a written statement to the SSA waiving the right to charge and collect a fee and expenses from a claimant or auxiliary beneficiary.

Fee Approval Process

In order to charge a fee, the representative must obtain SSA approval by filing a fee petition or fee agreement with the SSA. A representative may not file a fee petition for services in a claim if the SSA has approved a fee agreement and has authorized a fee under that approved agreement. The fee agreement and the fee petition processes are not interchangeable. Nevertheless, in either case, the representative cannot charge more than the approved fee amount.

A representative who charges or collects a fee without SSA approval, or charges or collects too much, may be suspended or disqualified from representing anyone before the SSA, and also may face criminal prosecution and is subject to fines and imprisonment.

If a third party will be paying the fee for the claimant, e.g., an insurance company, the SSA must still approve the fee unless:

1. It is a nonprofit organization or federal, state, county or city agency that will pay the fee and any expenses from government funds; and

2. The claimant's representative gives the SSA a written statement that the client will not have to pay any fee or expenses.

The Fee Petition

A fee petition is a written statement signed by a claimant's representative requesting the fee the representative wants to charge and collect for services he or she provided in pursuing the claimant's benefit rights in proceedings before the SSA. The fee petition details the services provided. the amount of time spent on the claim, and the fee amount being requested. The representative must give the claimant a copy of the fee petition.

The representative may file a fee petition when they have completed work on the claim. Based on this petition, SSA will authorize a reasonable fee for the specific services provided. A representative must file a fee petition to obtain SSA authorization if any of the following applies:

1. The representative and the claimant have no written fee agreement.

2. The representative filed a fee agreement, which the SSA did not approve.

3. The representative filed a fee agreement, which was initially approved, but subsequently, a reviewing official reversed the approval.

4. The representative filed a fee agreement which the SSA approved and, subsequently, the SSA disapproved that agreement because no past-due benefits resulted from the favorable determination or decision.

A representative may petition for fee approval by filing a Petition to Obtain Approval of a Fee for Representing a Claimant (SSA Form 1560) with the SSA. A sample petition is set forth at Appendix 23.

A representative may also petition for fee approval by providing in writing, all of the following information:

1. The dates the representative's services began and ended;

2. The specific services the representative provided;

3. The amount of time spent in each type of service;

4. The amount of the fee the representative wants to charge for the services;

5. The amount of the fee the representative wants to request or charge for services provided in the same matter before any State or Federal court;

6. The amount of money, if any, the representative received toward payment of the fee and has held in a trust or escrow account;

7. The amount(s) and a list of any expenses the representative incurred for which he or she has been paid or expects to be paid; and

8. A statement affirming that the representative has sent a copy of the petition and any attachments to the claimant.

In addition, the SSA may request a representative who is not an attorney to furnish a description of the special qualifications which enabled him or her to provide the claimant with valuable help.

A representative who is a legal guardian, committee, conservator, or other State Court appointed representative must also furnish copies of:

1. His or her fee request of the court;

2. His or her accounting to the court; and

3. Either the court's declination to order a fee, or the court's order of fees for his or her services as a legal guardian during the same period in which the representative provided services in proceedings before the SSA.

If the claimant disagrees with any of the information contained in the fee petition, he or she should contact the SSA within 20 days of receiving a copy. The SSA will review the fee petition, consider the reasonable value of the services provided by the representative, and will advise the claimant, in writing, of the fee amount approved.

Although a representative may file a fee petition at any SSA office, he or she generally files the petition with the office shown below:

If a court or the Appeals Council issued the decision, the representative sends the petition to:

Office of Hearings and Appeals, SSA
ATTN: Attorney Fee Branch, Suite 805
5107 Leesburg Pike
Falls Church, VA 22041-3255

If an Administrative Law Judge issued the decision, the representative sends the petition to him or her using the hearing office address.

In most other cases, the representative sends the petition to the processing center address that appears at the top right of the claimant's Title II notices, or in a Title XVI only case, to the servicing field office.

The Fee Agreement

If the claimant and the representative entered into a written fee agreement, a copy of the agreement must be provided to the SSA before they make a decision on the claim.

The Social Security Act does not require any specific language in a fee agreement. Therefore, representatives may write their own fee agreement language and the SSA will approve the agreement if it meets the statutory conditions of the Act and no exceptions apply. The SSA has written fee agreement model language that complies with the statutory conditions for approval of a fee agreement.

A Model Fee Agreement is set forth at Appendix 24.

The SSA will usually approve the agreement if: (a) both the claimant and representative signed it; (b) the agreed upon fee is the lesser of: (i) 25% of the claimant's past due benefits; or (ii) the amount set by the SSA and announced in the Federal Register (presently $5,300); (c) the SSA approves the claim(s); and (d) the claim results in past-due benefits.

However, because a fee agreement is a contract between a representative and his or her client, each fee agreement is unique, may appear in any form, and may include provisions in addition to the fee. For example, a fee agreement may contain additional provisions for payment of out-of-pocket expenses for medical reports, interest on an unpaid balance of an authorized fee, or for establishing a trust or escrow account, etc.

Representatives may use stamped or photocopied signatures in lieu of their actual signatures on a fee agreement, and may submit a photocopy or fax of the original fee agreement. A fee agreement stamped only with a representative's firm's name is not acceptable.

The SSA will advise the claimant, in writing, of the fee amount the representative can charge based on the agreement. A representative may accept payment in advance as long as he or she holds it in a trust or escrow account. If the SSA does not approve the fee agreement, they will advise the claimant and representative in writing, and the representative must file a fee petition to charge and collect a fee.

Fee Payment

The claimant will not owe the representative more than the approved fee unless the amount represents:

1. Any fee a Federal court allows for the representative's services before it; and

2. Out-of-pocket expenses the representative incurs or expects to incur, e.g., the cost of obtaining doctor's or hospital records. SSA approval is not required for such expenses.

If a representative charges the claimant more than the approved fee amount, the claimant should report this to the SSA.

DIRECT PAYMENT TO AN ATTORNEY REPRESENTATIVE

When the SSA authorizes a representative's fee based on an approved fee agreement or a fee petition, the SSA will withhold 25 percent of the claimant's Title II past-due benefits for payment of all or part of the authorized fee if:

1. At least one of the claimant's representatives is an attorney,

2. The claimant is entitled to past-due benefits under Title II, and

3. The attorney has not waived his or her fee or waived the right to direct payment.

When the SSA makes a direct payment to an attorney, the law requires the SSA to deduct a 6.3 percent assessment or "user fee" from the amount of the attorney fee payable from past-due benefits. This fee covers administrative costs. The attorney cannot charge or collect this expense from the claimant.

If the representative is an attorney, and it is determined that the claimant is owed past-due benefits, the SSA will usually withhold 25% of the claimant's past-due benefits to pay the representative on behalf of the claimant. The claimant must pay the representative any remainder of the fee owed over and above any amount held in escrow and any amount withheld by the SSA on behalf of the claimant and designated for the representative.

There is no provision for withholding past-due benefits towards direct payment of an authorized fee under Title XVI, or when the appointed representative is not an attorney. An appointed non-attorney representative, authorized a fee under the fee agreement or fee petition process, must collect the fee directly from the claimant.

Exceptions to the SSA Fee Approval Process

The only exceptions to the fee approval process are if the fee is for services provided:

1. When a nonprofit organization or government agency will pay the fee and any expenses from government funds and the claimant incurs no liability, directly or indirectly, for the cost(s);

2. In an official capacity such as legal guardian, committee, or similar court-appointed office and the court has approved the fee in question; or

3. In representing the claimant before a court of law. However, a representative who has provided services in a claim before both the Social Security Administration and a court of law may seek a fee from

either or both, but neither tribunal has the authority to set a fee for the other.

Fee Waiver

If the representative will not be charging a fee for their services, they must sign the waiver of fee section on the Appointment of Representative form.

ADMINISTRATIVE REVIEW PROCESS

When a claimant or representative disagrees with the SSA's determination to approve or disapprove a fee agreement, he or she may request administrative review of that determination. Under the fee agreement process only, the SSA decision maker may also request administrative review of the fee amount authorized. The party requesting administrative review must do so within 15 days of receiving the notice of the determination approving or disapproving the fee agreement or authorizing the amount of the fee.

When a claimant, affected auxiliary beneficiary, or representative disagrees with the amount of the fee the SSA authorized, he or she may also protest that determination by requesting an administrative review. Under the fee petition process, the party requesting administrative review must do so within 30 days after the date of the notice of the fee authorization.

CHAPTER 12:
SOCIAL SECURITY FRAUD

OFFICE OF THE INSPECTOR GENERAL

The Office of the Inspector General (OIG) is an independent law enforcement agency organized under the Social Security Administration (SSA) that investigates fraud in SSA programs, such as the Retirement, Survivors, Disability and Supplemental Security Income (SSI) programs. The OIG Office of Investigations (OI) investigates wrongdoing by applicants, beneficiaries, contractors, physicians, interpreters, representative payees, third parties, and SSA employees, and conducts joint investigations with other Federal, State and local law enforcement agencies.

TYPES OF FRAUDULENT ACTIVITY

Fraudulent activity may include:

1. False statements on claims;

2. Concealment of material facts or events affecting eligibility;

3. Misuse of benefits by a representative payee;

4. Buying or selling Social Security cards or SSA information;

5. Misuse of social security numbers involving people with links to terrorist groups or activities;

6. Crimes involving SSA employees;

7. Conflict of interest;

8. Fraud or misuse of grant or contracting funds;

9. Significant mismanagement and waste of funds; and

10. Standards of conduct violations.

THE FRAUD HOTLINE

The SSA operates a fraud hotline to receive reports of fraud, waste and abuse of SSA programs. Complaints may be made by telephone, mail, fax and e-mail. There is an online fraud reporting form available on the website, however, the SSA cannot guarantee confidentiality when fraud reports are transmitted through the internet where they may be accessed by third parties. If confidentiality is an issue, the complainant should send the report by fax or mail. A report may also be made anonymously.

Fraud reports may be mailed or faxed to:

The SSA Fraud Hotline
P.O. Box 17768
Baltimore, Maryland 21235
Fax: 410-597-0118
Tel: 1-800-269-0271/(TTY) 1-866-501-2101

Complainants should be prepared to provide the SSA with as much information as possible regarding the fraud allegation, including any identifying information regarding the suspect, such as their name, social security number, date of birth, address, and telephone number. If the fraudulent activity being reporting involves concealed work activity, it is important to include the name of the employer, employer`s address and phone number, and when the work activity began.

Once the fraud report has been made, the OIG does not provide information to the complainant concerning their investigation and/or the action they take regarding the allegations. The OIG will send the complainant an acknowledgement of the report, but will not communicate further with the complainant unless it is necessary to obtain information pertinent to the fraud investigation.

MISUSE OF BENEFITS BY A REPRESENTATIVE PAYEE

If it is alleged that a representative payee has misused the benefits being issued to a beneficiary, a fraud report should be filed immediately, and should include as much of the following information as is known:

1. The name of the representative payee;
2. The name of the beneficiary;
3. The social security number of the representative payee;
4. The social security number of the beneficiary;
5. The date of birth of the representative payee;
6. The date of birth of the beneficiary;

7. Details regarding the allegation, such as when the misuse occurred, how the misuse was committed, and where the misuse took place.

The SSA will take steps to investigate the matter and send the beneficiary a letter stating whether misuse has occurred or not. If the SSA finds that misuse has occurred, they will inform the beneficiary, in writing, whether they were negligent in appointing or monitoring the payee. If the SSA was negligent, they must pay the beneficiary whatever benefits were lost through payee misuse. If the SSA finds that they were not negligent, the beneficiary may appeal that decision.

MISUSE OF A SOCIAL SECURITY NUMBER

It is against the law to use someone else's social security number, or to give false information when applying for a number. It is also illegal to alter, buy or sell social security cards. Anyone convicted of these crimes is subject to fines and/or imprisonment. Unfortunately, Identity theft has become a widespread problem, and the misuse of a person's social security number can cause many problems for the victim.

Misuse for Credit Purposes

An individual may misuse someone's social security number to obtain credit. Thus, it is important to protect both your social security number and card. If you suspect that someone is misusing your social security number, you should report it to the Office of Inspector General Fraud Hotline.

Nevertheless, the SSA cannot fix the victim's credit record if their Social Security Number has been misused in this way. In addition, the Office of the Inspector General cannot place any type of fraud alert on an identity theft victim's social security number.

If someone misuses your social security number to obtain credit, you must contact the institution that authorized the credit and/or issued the credit card, as well as the major credit reporting agencies. Obtain a copy of your credit report and ask that an alert be placed on your credit record requiring that you be contacted before credit is extended using your name and SSN.

The three major credit reporting agencies are:

1. Equifax (Tel) 1-800-525-6285;

2. Trans Union (Tel) 1-800-680-7289; and

3. Experian (Tel) 1-888-397-3742.

In addition, you should also contact the Federal Trade Commission's Identity Theft Hotline at 1-877-IDTHEFT (1-877-438-4338). The FTC can also be reached at its website at www.ftc.gov. The FTC collects complaints about identity theft from those whose identities have been stolen. Although the FTC does not have the authority to bring criminal cases, the FTC can help victims of identity theft by providing information to assist them in resolving the financial and other problems that can result from this crime. The FTC puts your information into a secure consumer fraud database and may, in appropriate instances, share it with other law enforcement agencies and private entities, including any companies about which you may complain.

You should work with each credit bureau, creditor, employer and government agency involved to remove inaccurate information from your records. You should continue checking your credit report annually for inaccuracies. Keep copies of your correspondence, records of your telephone calls and other documents verifying your efforts to correct the problem.

Misuse for Federal Tax Purposes

If someone misuses your social security number on their federal tax returns, e.g., if the IRS has notified you that your refund cannot be processed because someone else has already used your social security number on their tax return, you should contact the IRS at 1-800-829-1040.

Misuse for Work Purposes

Some individuals will use another's social security number for work purposes. You can determine if someone is using your SSN for work purposes by completing a request for your Social Security Earnings Statement, which must be completed and returned to the SSA. It takes approximately four to six weeks to receive the statement from the time it is requested. If there are earnings posted to your record that do not belong to you, you should contact the SSA and have those earnings removed. This situation is known as "scrambled earnings."

EMPLOYER'S FAILURE TO WITHHOLD SOCIAL SECURITY TAX

If you receive a W-2 statement from your employer and it does not reflect withholdings, you should immediately contact the SSA and provide them with the information that is reflected on the W-2 statement. You may also take your W-2 statement to the local SSA office and they will take corrective action.

If you do not have a W-2 statement and are concerned that your employer is improperly withholding or failing to withhold Social Security, federal income or employment taxes, you should report this matter directly to the Internal Revenue Service (800-829-1040). Employers may be subject to criminal sanctions for willfully failing to pay employment taxes.

PROTECTING YOUR SOCIAL SECURITY NUMBER

It is important to protect the privacy of your social security number to prevent its misuse. The SSA suggests taking the following steps in order to protect yourself:

1. Keep your number and card in a safe place to prevent their theft.

2. Show your card to your employer voluntarily when you start a job, so your records are correct. Don't rely on your memory.

3. Check your name and Social Security number on your pay stub and W-2 form to make sure they are correct.

4. Notify the SSA every time you change your name.

If a business requests your social security number, you may refuse to give it to them. However, refusal may mean that the business will not provide the service offered. For example, an individual may apply for a store credit card. In that connection, the credit grantor may request the applicant's social security number. If the applicant refuses to supply their social security number, the credit grantor may refuse to issue the credit card.

If a business requests your social security number, you should inquire as to: (i) why it is needed; (ii) how it is going to be used; (iii) what law, if any, requires you to supply your social security number; and (iv) the consequences if you refuse to supply your social security number.

OBTAINING A NEW SOCIAL SECURITY NUMBER

Under certain circumstances, the Social Security Administration will assign a new social security number to a person who can document that they have been victimized and disadvantaged by the misuse of their social security number by another.

Nevertheless, a new SSN will not be assigned if an individual:

1. Is trying to avoid the law or their legal responsibility.

2. Intends to avoid disclosure of a poor credit or criminal record when they are at fault.

3. Has no proof that someone else caused the problem.

4. Has lost their social security card or it was stolen but there is no evidence that their SSN is being misused and that they are being disadvantaged.

PRIVACY OF SOCIAL SECURITY RECORDS

The SSA guarantees the privacy of an individual's social security records unless: (i) disclosure to another agency is required by law; or (ii) the information is needed to conduct Social Security or other government health or welfare programs. The SSA cannot prevent third parties from asking an individual for their social security number, and can't control the misuse of one's number once that individual gives it to someone. Nevertheless, giving your number to a third party does not give that person access to your Social Security records.

CHAPTER 13:
HEARINGS AND APPEALS

IN GENERAL

The Social Security Administration (SSA) considers all information on a claim before rendering a decision on eligibility or the amount of benefit. If the SSA decides that a person is not eligible, or is no longer eligible for benefits, or that the benefit amount is incorrect, they send the applicant a notice explaining their decision. If the applicant disagrees with the decision that the SSA has made on their application for benefits, they can request a review, called an "appeal."

The request for appeal must be made, in writing, within 60 days from the date the notice is received, plus an additional 5 days for mailing time. An extension of time to appeal may also be granted under certain circumstances. Pending the appeal, the applicant can obtain status on the case by contacting their local social security office, or the local hearing office, or by calling the SSA Division of Congressional and Public Inquiries staff (1-703-605-8000) or the general inquiries staff (1-800-772-1213).

LEVELS OF APPEAL

Reconsideration

A reconsideration is a complete review of the claim by someone other than the individual who made the original decision. All evidence, plus any additional evidence submitted, will be reevaluated and a new decision will be rendered.

If an individual disagrees with the reconsidered decision, they can choose to go to the next level of the appeals process—the hearing. It takes approximately 274 days to process a hearing request.

Hearing

Approximately 20 days before the hearing date, the claimant and their representative, if they have one, will receive a Notice of Hearing. The Notice contains a form asking if the claimant will be present at the hearing. This form must be returned as soon as possible.

The hearing is conducted by an Administrative Law Judge (ALJ). The individual and/or their representative are encouraged to come to the hearing and present their case in person. If the claimant cannot appear at the time of the hearing, they must notify their local SSA office.

In making his or her decision, the ALJ will evaluate all the evidence on record, plus any additional evidence brought to the hearing, and will render a decision. A "Notice of Decision" will be issued to the individual and their representative. After the ALJ renders a decision, the SSA takes approximately 30 days to send the detailed decision.

If an individual disagrees with the hearing decision, they can choose to go to the next level of appeal—the Appeals Council.

The Appeals Council

The Appeals Council is made up of approximately 27 Administrative Appeals Judges and 35 Appeals Officers, who must review and sign each final action. The Council receives about 100,000 requests for review each year and, as of September 2003, had a pending workload of 51,000 requests for review.

At the Appeals Council level, the claim file, request for review, and any additional evidence and/or comments submitted are assembled into a case folder by the support staff. Then a hearings and appeals analyst reviews the case folder. Hearings and appeals analysts are paralegal specialists, who have a great deal of experience in Social Security programs. The analyst prepares a written analysis of the case folder and a recommendation. He or she also prepares a notice, order, or decision for the Administrative Appeals Judge or Appeals Officer's signature.

The Administrative Appeals Judge or Appeals Officer considers the evidence, the hearing decision, the analysis, and recommendation. If the Judge or Officer agrees with the recommended action, he or she will sign the notice, order or decision. If they disagree, they may make appropriate changes or return the case folder to the analyst for a different action. The Administrative Appeals Judge or Appeals Officer issues the Appeals Council's action.

The average processing time for a request for review by the Appeals Council is approximately 7-1/2 months from the date the appeal is filed until the date the Council releases the final action. The request should be sent directly to the Appeals Council at 5107 Leesburg Pike, Falls Church, Virginia 22041-3255.

The Appeals Council may decide to issue its own decision, remand the case to the ALJ to issue another decision, or allow the ALJ's decision to stand. The appellant will receive a copy of the Appeals Council's action.

Federal Court Review

If the individual disagrees with the Appeals Council's action, or if the Appeals Council denies the claimant's request for a review, he or she has the right to file a civil suit in Federal District Court. Other claimant must commence the civil action by filing a complaint in the United States District Court for the judicial district in which they reside within sixty (60) days from the date they receive the Appeals Council's notice.

The complaint should name the Commissioner of Social Security as the defendant and should include the Social Security number(s) shown at the top of the denial notice. There is a charge for filing a civil action in Federal court. The claimant must file for civil action in a Federal District Court within 60 days of:

1. Receipt of the Appeals Council's notice of denial of the request for review of the ALJ's decision; or

2. Receipt of the Appeals Council's revised decision.

REPRESENTATION

Although many people handle their own appeals, they can choose a representative to assist them. The representative can be an attorney or non-attorney. The representative cannot charge or collect a fee without first obtaining approval from the SSA.

Representatives are discussed more fully in Chapter 11 of this almanac.

CHAPTER 14:
INTERNATIONAL ISSUES

NONCITIZENS

A noncitizen may receive Social Security benefits, however, the Personal Responsibility and Work Opportunity Reconciliation Act of 1996, (Public Law 104-193) permits payment of benefits to noncitizens living in the United States only if they are lawfully present in this country. The law requires that anyone living in the United States who applies for Social Security benefits on or after September 1, 1996, must provide evidence that he or she is a United States citizen or national, or an alien lawfully present in the United States as determined by the Attorney General.

This law does not affect:

1. Social Security benefits for people residing outside the U.S.;

2. Social Security benefits for people who applied before September 1, 1996; or

3. Entitlement to Medicare hospital insurance by a Social Security beneficiary.

UNITED STATES CITIZENS LIVING ABROAD

A United States citizen may receive their Social Security payments outside the United States as long as they are eligible for them. Regardless of citizenship, however, there are certain countries where the SSA is not allowed to send payments, e.g., Cambodia, Cuba, North Korea, Vietnam and many of the former U.S.S.R. republics (except Armenia, Estonia, Latvia, Lithuania and Russia). A complete list of those countries may be obtained by visiting the following website:

    http://www.socialsecurity.gov/international/your_ss.html

In several countries, personnel in the American embassies or consulates, and in the SSA Division of the Veterans Affairs Regional Office in Manila, Philippines, are specially trained to take applications for Social Security benefits.

Medicare

A United States citizen living abroad generally cannot benefit from the Medicare program because the program provides protection against the cost of hospital and medical expenses incurred in the United States.

There are rare emergency cases where Medicare can pay for care in Canada or Mexico. Also, Medicare can sometimes pay if a Canadian or Mexican hospital is closer to the recipient's home than the nearest U.S. hospital that can provide the care needed.

Health insurance protection may be very important to anyone temporarily abroad who plans to return to the United States. If an individual plans to return to the United States shortly after they are eligible for the medical insurance program, they may wish to enroll during the first enrollment period. If he or she expects to be abroad for a longer period of time, they may wish to enroll during a later general enrollment period. A general enrollment period is held January 1 through March 31 of each year, and protection will begin July 1 of the year the recipient enrolls.

NONCITIZENS LIVING ABROAD

If the recipient is not a United States citizen, the law requires the SSA to stop payments after the recipient has been outside the United States for six calendar months, unless they meet one of several exceptions in the law which will permit them to continue receiving benefits abroad.

These exceptions are based, for the most part, on the recipient's citizenship. For example, if he or she is entitled to worker's benefits and is a citizen of one of the many countries with which the United States has a reciprocal arrangement to pay each other's citizens in another country, the recipient's Social Security benefits may continue after they leave the United States. However, if the recipient works outside the United States, different rules apply in determining if the recipient can get benefit checks. Most people who are neither U.S. residents nor U.S. citizens will have 25.5 percent of their benefits withheld for federal income tax.

CREDIT FOR WORK PERFORMED ABROAD

Work overseas may help the applicant qualify for U.S. benefits if it was covered under a foreign Social Security system. The United States has Social Security agreements with a number of other countries. One of the main purposes of these agreements is to help people who have worked in both the United States and the other country, but who have not worked long enough in one country or the other to qualify for Social Security benefits. Under the agreement, the SSA can count the work credits in the other country if this will help the applicant qualify for U.S. benefits. However, if the applicant already has enough credits under U.S. Social Security to qualify for a benefit, the SSA will not count the credits in the other country.

If the SSA does count the applicant's foreign work credits, he or she will receive a partial U.S. benefit that is related to the length of time worked under U.S. Social Security. Although the SSA may count work credits in the other country, the applicant's credits are not actually transferred from that country to the United States. They remain on record in the other country. It is therefore possible for the applicant to qualify for a separate benefit payment from both countries.

ASSIGNING A SOCIAL SECURITY NUMBER TO A CHILD LIVING ABROAD

If a child lives outside the United States, the SSA can assign the child a Social Security number if the child is: (1) a U.S. citizen or (2) a noncitizen admitted to the United States for permanent residence ,or with other Department of Homeland Security (DHS) authority to work in the United States. Otherwise, the SSA will assign the child a number only if a Social Security number is required by law as a condition of receiving a federally-funded benefit.

The completed form should be taken or mailed with the required original documents, or copies certified by the custodian of the record, to the nearest U.S. Social Security office, U.S. Embassy or Consulate, or if the applicant lives in the Philippines, to the Veterans Affair Regional Office in Manila. If the applicant is a U.S. military dependent or a U.S. citizen working on a U.S. military post, the form may also be filed with the Post Adjutant or Personnel Office.

These offices can copy and certify the applicant's records so that they do not have to send original documents through the mail. The reader is advised not to mail original documents to the Social Security Administration in Baltimore, Maryland.

Once processed, the child's Social Security card will be mailed from the United States.

SPECIAL VETERANS BENEFITS

Special Veterans Benefits (SVB) are monthly payments made under title VIII of the Social Security Act to certain veterans of World War II who reside outside the United States. In order to receive Special Veterans Benefits, an individual must:

1. Be age 65 or older on December 14, 1999, the date the law was enacted;

2. Be a World War II veteran. This includes Filipino veterans of World War II who served in the organized military forces of the Philippines while the forces were in the service of the U.S. armed forces, or served in organized guerrilla forces under the auspices of the U.S. Military;

3. Be eligible for Supplemental Security Income (SSI) benefits for December 1999, the month the law was enacted;

4. File an application for SVB;

5. Be eligible for SSI benefits for the month in which he files an application for these new benefits; and

6. Have other benefit income that is less than 75 percent of the SSI Federal benefit rate.

An individual who meets all of these requirements can receive SVB for each month he or she resides outside the United States on the first day of the month. An individual is outside the United States if he or she is not in one of the 50 States, the District of Columbia or the Northern Mariana Islands.

GOVERNMENT WORKERS

Certain employees of federal, State and local government agencies and nonprofit organizations, and some individuals who have worked in other countries, may be eligible for pensions that are based on earnings not covered by Social Security. This can affect the amount of one's Social Security monthly benefits. The SSA does not know whether the applicant is eligible for such a pension before they apply for Social Security benefits.

OBTAINING ADDITIONAL INFORMATION

Individuals living outside of the United States can obtain more information by contacting the following: agencies depending on where they live:

1. Canada—Contact any U.S. Social Security office.

2. Guam, Puerto Rico, American Samoa or the U.S. Virgin Islands—Contact the nearest U.S. Social Security office.

3. Mexico—Contact any U.S. Social Security office or the nearest U.S. Embassy or consulate.

4. Philippines—Contact the SSA Division of the Veterans Affairs Regional Office.

Other Countries—If you live in any other country, contact the nearest U.S. Embassy or consulate.

An individual can continue to receive Special Veterans Benefits if they go to the United States for a visit and stay less than 1 full calendar month. For SVB purposes, an individual is in the United States if they are in one of the 50 States, the District of Columbia or the Northern Mariana Islands.

If the individual visits the United States and stays for more than a full calendar month, he or she will no longer be considered to be residing outside the United States for any month after the full calendar month they are in the United States. They will not be entitled to any SVB payments until they leave the United States and re-establish their residence outside the United States.

If the individual returns to the United States to live, they will not be entitled to a Special Veterans Benefits payment for any month after the month in which they leave their home outside the United States.

APPENDIX 1:
SOCIAL SECURITY ADMINISTRATION—
REGIONAL OFFICES

REGIONAL OFFICE	AREAS COVERED
ATLANTA (REGION 1)	Alabama, Florida, Georgia, Kentucky, Mississippi, North Carolina, South Carolina, Tennessee
BOSTON (REGION 2)	Connecticut, Maine, Massachusetts, New Hampshire, Rhode Island, Vermont
CHICAGO (REGION 3)	Illinois, Indiana, Michigan, Minnesota, Ohio, Wisconsin
DALLAS (REGION 4)	Arkansas, Louisiana, Oklahoma, New Mexico, Texas
DENVER (REGION 5)	Colorado, Montana, North Dakota, South Dakota, Utah, Wyoming
KANSAS CITY (REGION 6)	Iowa, Kansas, Missouri, Nebraska
NEW YORK (REGION 7)	New York, New Jersey, Puerto Rico, Virgin Islands.
PHILADELPHIA (REGION 8)	Delaware, Maryland, Pennsylvania, Virginia, West Virginia, District of Columbia
SAN FRANCISCO (REGION 9)	Arizona, California, Hawaii, Nevada, American Samoa, Guam, Saipan
SEATTLE (REGION 10)	Alaska, Idaho, Oregon, Washington

Source: Social Security Administration.

APPENDIX 2:
TABLE OF TOTAL SOCIAL SECURITY
NUMBERS ISSUED (1936-1996)

YEAR	TOTAL SOCIAL SECURITY NUMBERS ISSUED (Thousands)
1936-1937	37,139
1938	6,304
1939	5,555
1940	5,227
1941	6,678
1942	7,637
1943	7,426
1944	4,537
1945	3,321
1946	3,022
1947	2,728
1948	2,720
1949	2,340
1950	2,891
1951	4,927
1952	4,363
1953	3,464
1954	2,743
1955	4,323
1956	4,376
1957	3,639
1958	2,920
1959	3,388

YEAR	TOTAL SOCIAL SECURITY NUMBERS ISSUED (Thousands)
1960	3,415
1961	3,370
1962	4,519
1963	8,617
1964	5,623
1965	6,131
1966	6,506
1967	5,920
1968	5,862
1969	6,289
1970	6,132
1971	6,401
1972	9,564
1973	10,038
1974	7,998
1975	8,164
1976	9,043
1977	7,724
1978	5,260
1979	5,213
1980	5,980
1981	5,581
1982	5,362
1983	6,699
1984	5,980
1985	5,720
1986	5,711
1987	11,621
1988	11,370
1989	8,049
1990	9,054
1991	7,509
1992	6,819

YEAR	TOTAL SOCIAL SECURITY NUMBERS ISSUED (Thousands)
1993	5,893
1994	5,816
1995	5,465
1996	5,533
TOTAL	381,000,000

Source: Social Security Administration.

APPENDIX 3:
SOCIAL SECURITY AREA NUMBERS BY
GEOGRAPHIC REGION

AREA NUMBER	GEOGRAPHIC REGION
001-003	New Hampshire
004-007	Maine
008-009	Vermont
010-034	Massachusetts
035-039	Rhode Island
040-049	Connecticut
050-134	New York
135-158	New Jersey
159-211	Pennsylvania
212-220	Maryland
221-222	Delaware
223-231	Virginia
232-236	West Virginia
232, 237-246	North Carolina
247-251	South Carolina
252-260	Georgia
261-267	Florida
268-302	Ohio
303-317	Indiana
318-361	Illinois
362-386	Michigan
387-399	Wisconsin
400-407	Kentucky

SOCIAL SECURITY AREA NUMBERS BY GEOGRAPHIC REGION

AREA NUMBER	GEOGRAPHIC REGION
408-415	Tennessee
416-424	Alabama
425-428	Mississippi
429-432	Arkansas
433-439	Louisiana
440-448	Oklahoma
449-467	Texas
468-477	Minnesota
478-485	Iowa
486-500	Missouri
501-502	North Dakota
503-504	South Dakota
505-508	Nebraska
509-515	Kansas
516-517	Montana
518-519	Idaho
520	Wyoming
521-524	Colorado
525	New Mexico
526-527	Arizona
528-529	Utah
530	Nevada
531-539	Washington
540-544	Oregon
545-573	California
574	Alaska
575-576	Hawaii
577-579	District of Columbia
580	Virgin Islands
580-584	Puerto Rico
585	New Mexico
586	Guam
586	American Samoa
586	Philippine Islands

AREA NUMBER	GEOGRAPHIC REGION
586	Northern Mariana Islands
587-588	Mississippi
589-595	Florida
596-599	Puerto Rico
600-601	Arizona
602-626	California
627-645	Texas
646-647	Utah
648-649	New Mexico
650-653	Wisconsin
700-728	Railroad Retirement Board
750-751	Hawaii
752-755	Mississippi
756-763	Tennessee

NOTE: Table is current as of 5/97. Some numbers are shown more than once because they have either been transferred from one State to another or divided for use among certain geographic locations.

Source: Social Security Administration.

APPENDIX 4:
APPLICATION FOR SOCIAL SECURITY CARD

SOCIAL SECURITY ADMINISTRATION
Application for a Social Security Card

Applying for a Social Security Card is easy AND it is free!

USE THIS APPLICATION TO APPLY FOR:
- An original Social Security card
- A duplicate Social Security card (same name and number)
- A corrected Social Security card (name change and same number)
- A change of information on your record other than your name (no card needed)

IMPORTANT: You MUST provide the required evidence or we cannot process the application. Follow the instructions below to provide the information and evidence we need.

STEP 1 Read pages 1 through 3 which explain how to complete the application and what evidence we need.

STEP 2 Complete and sign the application using BLUE or BLACK ink. Do not use pencil or other colors of ink. Please print legibly.

STEP 3 Submit the completed and signed application with all required evidence to any Social Security office.

HOW TO COMPLETE THIS APPLICATION
Most items on the form are self-explanatory. Those that need explanation are discussed below. The numbers match the numbered items on the form. If you are completing this form for someone else, please complete the items as they apply to that person.

2. Show the address where you can receive your card 10 to 14 days from now.

3. If you check "Legal Alien **Not** Allowed to Work," you need to provide a document from the government agency requiring your Social Security number that explains why you need a number and that you meet all of the requirements for the benefit or service except for the number. A State or local agency requirement must conform with Federal law.

   If you check "Other," you need to provide proof you are entitled to a federally-funded benefit for which a Social Security number is required as a condition for you to receive payment.

5. Providing race/ethnic information is voluntary. However, if you do give us this information, it helps us prepare statistical reports on how Social Security programs affect people. We do not reveal the identities of individuals.

6. Show the month, day and full (4 digit) year of birth, for example, "1998" for year of birth.

8.B. Show the mother's Social Security number only if you are applying for an original Social Security card for a child under age 18. You may leave this item blank if the mother does not have a number or you do not know the mother's number. We will still be able to assign a number to the child.

9.B. Show the father's Social Security number only if you are applying for an original Social Security card for a child under age 18. You may leave this item blank if the father does not have a number or you do not know the father's number. We will still be able to assign a number to the child.

13. If the date of birth you show in item 6 is different from the date of birth you used on a prior application for a Social Security card, show the date of birth you used on the prior application and submit evidence of age to support the date of birth in item 6.

16. You **must** sign the application yourself if you are age 18 or older and are physically and mentally capable. If you are under age 18, you may also sign the application if you are physically and mentally capable. If you cannot sign your name, you should sign with an "X" mark and have two people sign as witnesses in the space beside the mark. If you are physically or mentally incapable of signing the application, generally a parent, close relative, or legal guardian may sign the application. Call us if you need clarification about who can sign.

ABOUT YOUR DOCUMENTS

* We need **ORIGINAL** documents or **copies certified by the custodian of the record.** We will return your documents after we have seen them.

* **We cannot accept photocopies or notarized copies of documents.**

* If your documents do not meet this requirement, we cannot process your application.

DOCUMENTS WE NEED

To apply for an **ORIGINAL CARD** (you have NEVER been assigned a Social Security number before), we need at least 2 documents as proof of:

* **Age,**
* **Identity, and**
* **U.S. citizenship or lawful alien status.**

To apply for a **DUPLICATE CARD** (same number, same name), we need proof of **identity.**

To apply for a **CORRECTED CARD** (same number, different name), we need proof of **identity.** We need one or more documents which identify you by the OLD NAME on our records and your NEW NAME. Examples include: a marriage certificate, divorce decree, or a court order that changes your name. Or we can accept two identity documents - one in your old name and one in your new name. (See IDENTITY, for examples of identity documents.)

IMPORTANT: If you are applying for a duplicate or corrected card and were **born outside the U.S.,** we also need proof of U.S. citizenship or lawful alien status. (See U.S. CITIZENSHIP or ALIEN STATUS for examples of documents you can submit.)

AGE: We prefer to see your birth certificate. However, we can accept another document that shows your age. Some of the other documents we can accept are:

* Hospital record of your birth (created at the time of your birth)
* Religious record showing your age made before you were 3 months old
* Passport
* Adoption record (the adoption record must indicate that the birth data was taken from the original birth certificate)

Call us for advice if you cannot obtain one of these documents.

IDENTITY: We must see a document in the name you want shown on the card. The identity document must be of recent issuance so that we can determine your continued existence. We prefer to see a document with a photograph. However, we can generally accept a non-photo identity document if it has enough information to identify you (e.g., your name, as well as age, date of birth or parents' names). **WE CANNOT ACCEPT A BIRTH CERTIFICATE, HOSPITAL SOUVENIR BIRTH CERTIFICATE, SOCIAL SECURITY CARD OR CARD STUB, OR SOCIAL SECURITY RECORD** as evidence of identity. Some documents we can accept are:

- Driver's license
- Employee ID card
- Passport

- Marriage or divorce record
- Adoption record (only if not being used to establish age)
- Health insurance card (not a Medicare card)

- Military record
- Life insurance policy
- School ID card

As evidence of identity for infants and young children, we can accept :

- Doctor, clinic, hospital record
- Daycare center, school record
- Religious record (e.g., baptismal record)

IMPORTANT: If you are **applying for a card on behalf of someone else,** you must provide evidence that establishes your authority to sign the application on behalf of the person to whom the card will be issued. In addition, we must see proof of identity for both you and the person to whom the card will be issued.

U. S. CITIZENSHIP: We can accept most documents that show you were born in the U.S. If you are a U.S. citizen born outside the U.S., show us a U.S. consular report of birth, a U.S. passport, a Certificate of Citizenship, or a Certificate of Naturalization.

ALIEN STATUS: We need to see an unexpired document issued to you by the Department of Homeland Security (DHS) showing your immigration status, such as Form I-551, I-94, I-688B, or I-766. We CANNOT accept a receipt showing you applied for the document. If you are not authorized to work in the U.S., we can issue you a Social Security card if you are lawfully here and need the number for a valid nonwork reason. (See HOW TO COMPLETE THIS APPLICATION, Item 3.) Your card will be marked to show you cannot work. If you do work, we will notify DHS.

To **CHANGE INFORMATION** on your record other than your name, we need proof of:

- **Identity,** and
- **Another document which supports the change** (for example, a birth certificate to change your date and/or place of birth or parents' names).

HOW TO SUBMIT THIS APPLICATION

In most cases, you can mail this application with your evidence documents to any Social Security office. We will return your documents to you. If you do not want to mail your original documents, take them with this application to the nearest Social Security office.

EXCEPTION: If you are age 12 or older and have never been assigned a number before, you must apply in person.

If you have any questions about this form, or about the documents we need, please contact any Social Security office. A telephone call will help you make sure you have everything you need to apply for a card or change information on your record. You can find your nearest office in your local phone directory or on our website at www.socialsecurity.gov.

THE PAPERWORK/PRIVACY ACT AND YOUR APPLICATION

The Privacy Act of 1974 requires us to give each person the following notice when applying for a Social Security number.

Sections 205(c) and 702 of the Social Security Act allow us to collect the facts we ask for on this form.

We use the facts you provide on this form to assign you a Social Security number and to issue you a Social Security card. You do not have to give us these facts, however, without them we cannot issue you a Social Security number or a card. Without a number, you may not be able to get a job and could lose Social Security benefits in the future.

The Social Security number is also used by the Internal Revenue Service for tax administration purposes as an identifier in processing tax returns of persons who have income which is reported to the Internal Revenue Service and by persons who are claimed as dependents on someone's Federal income tax return.

We may disclose information as necessary to administer Social Security programs, including to appropriate law enforcement agencies to investigate alleged violations of Social Security law; to other government agencies for administering entitlement, health, and welfare programs such as Medicaid, Medicare, veterans benefits, military pension, and civil service annuities, black lung, housing, student loans, railroad retirement benefits, and food stamps; to the Internal Revenue Service for Federal tax administration; and to employers and former employers to properly prepare wage reports. We may also disclose information as required by Federal law, for example, to the Department of Homeland Security, to identify and locate aliens in the U.S.; to the Selective Service System for draft registration; and to the Department of Health and Human Services for child support enforcement purposes. We may verify Social Security numbers for State motor vehicle agencies that use the number in issuing drivers licenses, as authorized by the Social Security Act. Finally, we may disclose information to your Congressional representative if they request information to answer questions you ask him or her.

We may use the information you give us when we match records by computer. Matching programs compare our records with those of other Federal, State, or local government agencies to determine whether a person qualifies for benefits paid by the Federal government. The law allows us to do this even if you do not agree to it.

Explanations about these and other reasons why information you provide us may be used or given out are available in Social Security offices. If you want to learn more about this, contact any Social Security office.

This information collection meets the requirements of 44 U.S.C. §3507, as amended by Section 2 of the Paperwork Reduction Act of 1995. You do not need to answer these questions unless we display a valid Office of Management and Budget control number. We estimate that it will take about 8.5 to 9 minutes to read the instructions, gather the facts, and answer the questions. **SEND THE COMPLETED FORM TO YOUR LOCAL SOCIAL SECURITY OFFICE.** The office is listed under U. S. Government agencies in your telephone directory or you may call Social Security at 1-800-772-1213. *You may send comments on our time estimate above to: SSA, 1338 Annex Building, Baltimore, MD 21235-0001. Send only comments relating to our time estimate to this address, not the completed form.*

Form SS-5 (10-2003) EF (10-2003)   Page 4

SOCIAL SECURITY ADMINISTRATION
Application for a Social Security Card

Form Approved
OMB No. 0960-0066

1	NAME TO BE SHOWN ON CARD	First	Full Middle Name	Last
	FULL NAME AT BIRTH IF OTHER THAN ABOVE	First	Full Middle Name	Last
	OTHER NAMES USED			

2	MAILING ADDRESS Do Not Abbreviate	Street Address, Apt. No., PO Box, Rural Route No.		
		City	State	Zip Code

3 CITIZENSHIP (Check One) — ☐ U.S. Citizen ☐ Legal Alien Allowed To Work ☐ Legal Alien Not Allowed To Work (See Instructions On Page 1) ☐ Other (See Instructions On Page 1)

4 SEX — ☐ Male ☐ Female

5 RACE/ETHNIC DESCRIPTION (Check One Only - Voluntary) — ☐ Asian, Asian-American or Pacific Islander ☐ Hispanic ☐ Black (Not Hispanic) ☐ North American Indian or Alaskan Native ☐ White (Not Hispanic)

6 DATE OF BIRTH _____ Month, Day, Year

7 PLACE OF BIRTH (Do Not Abbreviate) _____ City _____ State or Foreign Country   FCI   Office Use Only

8	A. MOTHER'S MAIDEN NAME	First	Full Middle Name	Last Name At Her Birth
	B. MOTHER'S SOCIAL SECURITY NUMBER	☐☐☐–☐☐–☐☐☐☐		

9	A. FATHER'S NAME	First	Full Middle Name	Last
	B. FATHER'S SOCIAL SECURITY NUMBER	☐☐☐–☐☐–☐☐☐☐		

10 Has the applicant or anyone acting on his/her behalf ever filed for or received a Social Security number card before?
☐ Yes (If "yes", answer questions 11-13.) ☐ No (If "no", go on to question 14.) ☐ Don't Know (If "don't know", go on to question 14.)

11 Enter the Social Security number previously assigned to the person listed in item 1. → ☐☐☐–☐☐–☐☐☐☐

12 Enter the name shown on the most recent Social Security card issued for the person listed in item 1. ——— First   Middle Name   Last

13 Enter any different date of birth if used on an earlier application for a card. ——— Month, Day, Year

14 TODAY'S DATE _____ Month, Day, Year

15 DAYTIME PHONE NUMBER ( ) _____ Area Code   Number

I declare under penalty of perjury that I have examined all the information on this form, and on any accompanying statements or forms, and it is true and correct to the best of my knowledge.

16 YOUR SIGNATURE ▶

17 YOUR RELATIONSHIP TO THE PERSON IN ITEM 1 IS:
☐ Self ☐ Natural Or Adoptive Parent ☐ Legal Guardian ☐ Other (Specify)

DO NOT WRITE BELOW THIS LINE (FOR SSA USE ONLY)

NPN		DOC	NTI	CAN		ITV
PBC	EVI	EVA	EVC	PRA	NWR	DNR	UNIT

EVIDENCE SUBMITTED

SIGNATURE AND TITLE OF EMPLOYEE(S) REVIEWING EVIDENCE AND/OR CONDUCTING INTERVIEW

DATE

DCL

DATE

Form SS-5 (10-2003) EF (10-2003) Destroy Prior Editions   Page 5

APPENDIX 5:
REQUEST FOR SOCIAL SECURITY STATEMENT

Form Approved
OMB No. 0960-0466

SP

Request for Social Security Statement

☐ Please check this box if you want to get your *Statement* in Spanish instead of English.

Please print or type your answers. When you have completed the form, fold it and mail it to us. (If you prefer to send your request using the Internet, contact us at *www.socialsecurity.gov*)

1. Name shown on your Social Security card:

First Name

Middle Initial

Last Name Only

2. Your Social Security number as shown on your card:

☐☐☐ - ☐☐ - ☐☐☐☐

3. Your date of birth (Mo.-Day-Yr.):

☐☐ - ☐☐ - ☐☐☐☐

4. Other Social Security numbers you have used:

☐☐☐ - ☐☐ - ☐☐☐☐
☐☐☐ - ☐☐ - ☐☐☐☐

5. Your Sex: ☐ Male   ☐ Female

For items 6 and 8 show only earnings covered by Social Security. Do NOT include wages from state, local or federal government employment that are NOT covered for Social Security or that are covered ONLY by Medicare.

6. Show your actual earnings (wages and/or net self-employment income) for last year and your estimated earnings for this year.

A. Last year's actual earnings: *(Dollars Only)*

$ ☐☐☐ , ☐☐☐ ☐☐

B. This year's estimated earnings: *(Dollars Only)*

$ ☐☐☐ , ☐☐☐ ☐☐

7. Show the age at which you plan to stop working.

☐ *(Show only one age)*

8. Below, show the average yearly amount (not your total future lifetime earnings) that you think you will earn between now and when you plan to stop working. Include performance or scheduled pay increases or bonuses, but not cost-of-living increases.

If you expect to earn significantly more or less in the future due to promotions, job changes, part-time work, or an absence from the work force, enter the amount that most closely reflects your future average yearly earnings.

If you don't expect any significant changes, show the same amount you are earning now (the amount in 6B).

Future average yearly earnings: *(Dollars Only)*

$ ☐☐☐ , ☐☐☐ ☐☐

9. Do you want us to send the *Statement*:
   • To you? Enter your name and mailing address.
   • To someone else (your accountant, pension plan, etc.)? Enter your name with "c/o" and the name and address of that person or organization.

"C/O" or Street Address (Include Apt. No.; P.O. Box, Rural Route)

Street Address

Street Address (If Foreign Address, enter City, Province, Postal Code)

U.S. City, State, Zip code (If Foreign Address, enter Name of Country only)

NOTICE:
I am asking for information about my own Social Security record or the record of a person I am authorized to represent. I declare under penalty of perjury that I have examined all the information on this form, and on any accompanying statements or forms, and it is true and correct to the best of my knowledge. I authorize you to use a contractor to send the *Social Security Statement* to the person and address in item 9.

▲

Please sign your name (Do Not Print)

Date _____

(Area Code) Daytime Telephone No.

Form SSA-7004-SM (1-2003) EF (01-2003)
Destroy prior editions

SOCIAL SECURITY ADMINISTRATION

Request for *Social Security* *Statement*

After you complete and return this form, within 4 to 6 weeks we will send you:

- a record of your earnings history and an estimate of how much you have paid in Social Security taxes, and
- estimates of benefits you (and your family) may be eligible for now and in the future.

We're pleased to furnish you with this information and we hope you'll find it useful in planning your financial future.

Social Security is more than just a program for retired people. It helps people of all ages in many ways. Whether you're young or old, male or female, single or married, Social Security can help you when you need it most. It can help support your family in the event of your death and pay you benefits if you become severely disabled.

If you have questions about Social Security or this form, please call our toll-free number, **1-800-772-1213.**

About The Privacy Act

Social Security is allowed to collect the facts on this form under section 205 of the Social Security Act. We need them to quickly identify your record and prepare the *Statement* you asked us for. Giving us these facts is voluntary. However, without them we may not be able to give you a *Statement*. Neither the Social Security Administration nor its contractor will use the information for any other purpose.

Paperwork Reduction Act Notice

This information collection meets the requirements of 44 U.S.C. §3507, as amended by Section 2 of the Paperwork Reduction Act of 1995. You do not need to answer these questions unless we display a valid Office of Management and Budget control number. We estimate that it will take about 5 minutes to read the instructions, gather the facts, and answer the questions. **SEND THE COMPLETED FORM TO YOUR LOCAL SOCIAL SECURITY OFFICE. The office is listed under U. S. Government agencies in your telephone directory or you may call Social Security at 1-800-772-1213.** *You may send comments on our time estimate above to: SSA, 1338 Annex Building, Baltimore, MD 21235-0001. Send only comments relating to our time estimate to this address, not the completed form.*

APPENDIX 6:
NUMBER OF RETIRED WORKERS AND THEIR DEPENDENTS RECEIVING BENEFITS (1970-2003)

AGE	TOTAL
1970	16,566,674
1971	17,188,035
1972	17,870,175
1973	18,793,039
1974	19,409,560
1975	20,140,731
1976	20,715,021
1977	21,476,517
1978	22,006,468
1979	22,617,898
1980	23,243,078
1981	23,859,047
1982	24,362,481
1983	24,971,472
1984	25,435,753
1985	25,958,585
1986	26,524,806
1987	26,970,080
1988	27,375,814
1989	27,842,330
1990	28,361,385
1991	28,818,483

AGE	TOTAL
1992	29,301,178
1993	29, 635,117
1994	29,914,265
1995	30,140,418
1996	30,310,865
1997	30,637,863
1998	30,813,491
1999	31,027,701
2000	31,756,099
2001	32,045,800
2002	32,347,974
2003	32,633,335

Source: Social Security Administration.

APPENDIX 7:
LIFE EXPECTANCY TABLES, REMAINING YEARS OF LIFE BASED ON AGE, ALL RACES, 1996

AGE	BOTH SEXES	MALE	FEMALE
0	76.1	73.0	79.0
1	75.6	72.6	78.6
5	71.7	68.7	74.7
10	66.8	63.8	69.7
15	61.9	58.9	64.8
20	57.1	54.2	59.9
25	52.4	49.6	55.1
30	47.7	44.9	50.2
35	43.0	40.4	45.4
40	38.4	35.9	40.7
45	33.9	31.5	36.0
50	29.4	27.1	31.5
55	25.2	23.0	27.1
60	21.2	19.2	22.9
65	17.5	15.7	18.9
70	14.1	12.5	15.3
75	11.1	9.8	11.9
80	8.3	7.3	8.9
85	6.1	5.4	6.4

Source: United States Department of Health.

APPENDIX 8:
AVERAGE REMAINING LIFE EXPECTANCY
FOR INDIVIDUALS SURVIVING TO AGE 65
(1940-1990)

YEAR	MALE	FEMALE
1940	12.7	13.1
1950	13.2	13.8
1960	14.6	15.3
1970	14.7	16.2
1980	17.4	18.6
1990	19.1	19.6

Source: Social Security Administration.

APPENDIX 9:
ELIGIBILITY AGE FOR FULL SOCIAL SECURITY BENEFITS ACCORDING TO YEAR OF BIRTH

YEAR OF BIRTH	FULL RETIREMENT AGE
1937 or earlier	65
1938	65 and 2 months
1939	65 and 4 months
1940	65 and 6 months
1941	65 and 8 months
1942	65 and 10 months
1943-1954	66
1955	66 and 2 months
1956	66 and 4 months
1957	66 and 6 months
1958	66 and 8 months
1959	66 and 10 months
1960 and later	67

Source: Social Security Administration.

APPENDIX 10:
PERCENTAGE OF INCREASE IN SOCIAL SECURITY BENEFITS FOR EACH YEAR OF DELAYED RETIREMENT BEYOND FULL RETIREMENT AGE

YEAR OF BIRTH	YEARLY RATE OF INCREASE
1917-1924	3%
1925-1926	3.5%
1927-1928	4%
1929-1930	4.5%
1931-1932	5%
1933-1934	5.5%
1935-1936	6%
1937-1938	6.5%
1939-1940	7%
1941-1942	7.5%
1943 or later	8%

Source: Social Security Administration.

APPENDIX 11:
SOCIAL SECURITY COST OF LIVING ALLOWANCE (COLA) INCREASES (1950-2003)

EFFECTIVE DATE	PERCENT INCREASE
9/50	77.0
9/52	12.5
9/54	13.0
1/59	7.0
1/65	7.0
2/68	13.0
1/70	15.0
1/71	10.0
9/72	20.0
3/74*	7.0*
6/74	11.0
6/75	8.0
6/76	6.4
6/77	5.9
6/78	6.5
6/79	9.9
6/80	14.3
6/81	11.2
6/82	7.4
12/83	3.5
12/84	3.5
12/85	3.1

SOCIAL SECURITY COST OF LIVING ALLOWANCE (COLA) INCREASES

EFFECTIVE DATE	PERCENT INCREASE
12/86	1.3
12/87	4.2
12/88	4.0
12/89	4.7
12/90	5.4
12/91	3.7
12/92	3.0
12/93	2.6
12/94	2.8
12/95	2.6
12/96	2.9
12/97	2.1
12/98	1.3
12/99	2.5
12/00	3.5
12/01	2.6
12/02	1.4
12/03	2.1

*Note: The increase in 3/74 was a special, limited-duration increase. It was effective for only 3/74-5/74. In June 1974 all payment levels reverted to their 2/74 level and the 11% increase was permanently applied on this base. The COLA for December 1999 was originally determined as 2.4 percent based on the consumer price index published by the Bureau of Labor Statistics. Pursuant to Public Law 106-554, however, this COLA is effectively now 2.5 percent.

Source: Social Security Administration.

APPENDIX 12:
NUMBER OF DISABLED WORKERS AND THEIR DEPENDENTS RECEIVING BENEFITS (1970-2003)

1970	2,665,629
1971	2,929,900
1972	3,271,486
1973	3,560,706
1974	3,911,951
1975	4,352,498
1976	4,623,827
1977	4,854,206
1978	4,868,576
1979	4,777,218
1980	4,682,172
1981	4,456,274
1982	3,973,465
1983	3,812,930
1984	3,821,804
1985	3,907,169
1986	3,993,279
1987	4,044,724
1988	4,074,300
1989	4,128,827
1990	4,265,981
1991	4,513,040
1992	4,889,696
1993	5,253,566

1994	5,583,519
1995	5,857,656
1996	6,072,034
1997	6,153,039
1998	6,334,570
1999	6,523,730
2000	6,673,362
2001	6,913,243
2002	7,221,268
2003	7,595,452

Source: Social Security Administration.

APPENDIX 13:
AUTHORIZATION TO
DISCLOSE INFORMATION

Form Approved
OMB No. 0960-0623

WHOSE *Records to be Disclosed*

	First	Middle	Last

NAME

SSN   Birthday (mm/dd/yy)

SSA USE ONLY NUMBER HOLDER (If other than above)

NAME

SSN

AUTHORIZATION TO DISCLOSE INFORMATION TO
THE SOCIAL SECURITY ADMINISTRATION (SSA)
** PLEASE READ THE ENTIRE FORM, BOTH PAGES, BEFORE SIGNING BELOW **

I voluntarily authorize and request disclosure (including paper, oral, and electronic interchange):

OF WHAT *All my medical records;* also education records and other information related to my ability to perform tasks. This includes specific permission to release:

1. All records and other information regarding my treatment, hospitalization, and outpatient care for my impairment(s) *including,* and not limited to:
   - Psychological, psychiatric or other mental impairment(s) (excludes "psychotherapy notes" as defined in 45 CFR 164.501)
   - Drug abuse, alcoholism, or other substance abuse
   - Sickle cell anemia
   - Human immunodeficiency virus (HIV) infection (including acquired immunodeficiency syndrome (AIDS) or tests for HIV) or sexually transmitted diseases
   - Gene-related impairments (including genetic test results)
2. Information about how my impairment(s) affects my ability to complete tasks and activities of daily living, and affects my ability to work.
3. Copies of educational tests or evaluations, including Individualized Educational Programs, triennial assessments, psychological and speech evaluations, and any other records that can help evaluate function; also teachers' observations and evaluations.
4. Information created within 12 months after the date this authorization is signed, as well as past information.

FROM WHOM
- All medical sources (hospitals, clinics, labs, physicians, psychologists, etc.) including mental health, correctional, addiction treatment, and VA health care facilities
- All educational sources (schools, teachers, records administrators, counselors, etc.)
- Social workers/rehabilitation counselors
- Consulting examiners used by SSA
- Employers
- Others who may know about my condition (family, neighbors, friends, public officials)

THIS BOX TO BE COMPLETED BY SSA/DDS (as needed) Additional information to identify the subject (e.g., other names used), the specific source, or the material to be disclosed:

TO WHOM The Social Security Administration and to the State agency authorized to process my case (usually called "disability determination services"), including contract copy services, and doctors or other professionals consulted during the process. (Also, for international claims, to the U.S. Department of State Foreign Service Post.)

PURPOSE Determining my eligibility for benefits, including looking at the combined effect of any impairments that by themselves would not meet SSA's definition of disability; and whether I can manage such benefits.

☐ Determining whether I am capable of managing benefits ONLY (check only if applies)

EXPIRES WHEN This authorization is good for 12 months from the date signed (below my signature).

- I authorize the use of a copy (including electronic copy) of this form for the disclosure of the information described above.
- I understand that there are some circumstances in which this information may be redisclosed to other parties (see page 2 for details).
- I may write to SSA and my sources to revoke this authorization at any time (see page 2 for details).
- SSA will give me a copy of this form if I ask; I may ask the source to allow me to inspect or get a copy of material to be disclosed.
- I have read both pages of this form and agree to the disclosures above from the types of sources listed.

INDIVIDUAL authorizing disclosure

IF not signed by subject of disclosure, specify basis for authority to sign

☐ Parent of minor   ☐ Guardian   ☐ Other personal representative (explain)

SIGN ▶

(Parent/guardian/personal representative sign ▶ here if two signatures required by State law)

Date Signed	Street Address		
Phone Number (with area code)	City	State	ZIP

WITNESS *I know the person signing this form or am satisfied of this person's identity:*

SIGN ▶

IF needed, second witness sign here (e.g., if signed with "X" above)

SIGN ▶

Phone Number (or Address) | Phone Number (or Address)

This general and special authorization to disclose was developed to comply with the provisions regarding disclosure of medical, educational, and other information under P.L. 104-191 ("HIPAA"); 45 CFR parts 160 and 164; 42 U.S. Code section 290dd-2; 42 CFR part 2; 38 U.S. Code section 7332; 38 CFR 1.475; 20 U.S. Code section 1232g ("FERPA"); 34 CFR parts 99 and 300; and State law.

Form **SSA-827** (7-2003)   EF (07-2003)   Prior 2-2003 Edition Usable   Page 1 of 2

AUTHORIZATION TO DISCLOSED INFORMATION

Explanation of Form SSA-827,
"Authorization to Disclose Information to the Social Security Administration (SSA)"

We need your written authorization to help get the information required to process your application for benefits, and to determine your capability of managing benefits. Laws and regulations require that sources of personal information have a signed authorization before releasing it to us. Also, laws require specific authorization for the release of information about certain conditions and from educational sources.

You can provide this authorization by signing a Form SSA-827. Federal law permits sources with information about you to release that information if you sign a single authorization to release all your information from all your possible sources. We will make copies of it for each source. A few States, and some individual sources of information, require that the authorization specifically name the source that you authorize to release personal information. In those cases, we may ask you to sign one authorization for each source and we may contact you again if we need you to sign more authorizations.

You have the right to revoke this authorization at any time, except to the extent a source of information has already relied on it to take an action. To revoke, send a written statement to any Social Security Office. If you do, also send a copy directly to any of your sources that you no longer wish to disclose information about you; SSA can tell you if we identified any sources you didn't tell us about. SSA may use information disclosed prior to revocation to decide your claim.

It is SSA's policy to provide service to people with limited English proficiency in their native language or preferred mode of communication consistent with Executive Order 13166 (August 11, 2000) and the Individuals with Disabilities Education Act. SSA makes every reasonable effort to ensure that the information in the SSA-827 is provided to you in your native or preferred language.

IMPORTANT INFORMATION, INCLUDING NOTICE REQUIRED BY THE PRIVACY ACT

All personal information SSA collects is protected by the Privacy Act of 1974. Once medical information is disclosed to SSA, it is no longer protected by the health information privacy provisions of 45 CFR part 164 (mandated by the Health Insurance Portability and Accountability Act (HIPAA)). SSA retains personal information in strict adherence to the retention schedules established and maintained in conjunction with the National Archives and Records Administration. At the end of a record's useful life cycle, it is destroyed in accordance with the privacy provisions, as specified in 36 CFR part 1228.

SSA is authorized to collect the information on form SSA-827 by sections 205(a), 223 (d)(5)(A),1614(a)(3)(H)(i), 1631(d)(1) and 1631 (e)(1)(A) of the Social Security Act. We use the information obtained with this form to determine your eligibility for benefits, and your ability to manage any benefits received. This use usually includes review of the information by the State agency processing your case and quality control people in SSA. In some cases, your information may also be reviewed by SSA personnel that process your appeal of a decision, or by investigators to resolve allegations of fraud or abuse, and may be used in any related administrative, civil, or criminal proceedings.

Signing this form is voluntary, but failing to sign it, or revoking it before we receive necessary information, could prevent an accurate or timely decision on your claim, and could result in denial or loss of benefits. Although the information we obtain with this form is almost never used for any purpose other than those stated above, the information may be disclosed by SSA without your consent if authorized by Federal laws such as the Privacy Act and the Social Security Act. For example, SSA may disclose information:

1. To enable a third party (e.g., consulting physicians) or other government agency to assist SSA to establish rights to Social Security benefits and/or coverage;
2. Pursuant to law authorizing the release of information from Social Security records (e.g., to the Inspector General, to Federal or State benefit agencies or auditors, or to the Department of Veterans Affairs (VA));
3. For statistical research and audit activities necessary to ensure the integrity and improvement of the Social Security programs (e.g., to the Bureau of the Census and private concerns under contract with SSA).

SSA will not redisclose without proper prior written consent information: (1) relating to alcohol and/or drug abuse as covered in 42 CFR part 2, or (2) from educational records for a minor obtained under 34 CFR part 99 (Family Educational Rights and Privacy Act (FERPA)), or (3) regarding mental health, developmental disability, AIDS or HIV.

We may also use the information you give us when we match records by computer. Matching programs compare our records with those of other Federal, State, or local government agencies. Many agencies may use matching programs to find or prove that a person qualifies for benefits paid by the Federal government. The law allows us to do this even if you do not agree to it.

Explanations about possible reasons why information you provide us may be used or given out are available upon request from any Social Security Office.

PAPERWORK REDUCTION ACT

This information collection meets the requirements of 44 U.S.C. § 3507, as amended by Section 2 of the Paperwork Reduction Act of 1995. You do not need to answer these questions unless we display a valid Office of Management and Budget control number. We estimate that it will take about 10 minutes to read the instructions, gather the facts, and answer the questions. SEND OR BRING IN THE COMPLETED FORM TO YOUR LOCAL SOCIAL SECURITY OFFICE. The office is listed under U. S. Government agencies in your telephone directory or you may call Social Security at 1-800-772-1213. You may send comments on our time estimate above to: SSA, 1338 Annex Building, Baltimore, MD 21235-0001. Send only comments relating to our time estimate to this address, not the completed form.

Form SSA-827 (7-2003)   EF (07-2003)   Page 2 of 2

APPENDIX 14:
NUMBER OF SURVIVORS RECEIVING
BENEFITS (1970-2003)

1970	6,468,621
1971	6,699,531
1972	6,933,998
1973	7,159,932
1974	7,254,228
1975	7,368,439
1976	7,496,649
1977	7,592,375
1978	7,577,983
1979	7,617,842
1980	7,600,836
1981	7,614,727
1982	7,441,849
1983	7,249,574
1984	7,181,017
1985	7,160,944
1986	7,165,349
1987	7,156,381
1988	7,162,789
1989	7,169,923
1990	7,197,326
1991	7,255,351
1992	7,312,632
1993	7,354,579
1994	7,384,066

1995	7,388,158
1996	7,353,284
1997	7,179,790
1998	7,097,445
1999	7,044,050
2000	6,985,244
2001	6,918,422
2002	6,875,054
2003	6,809,688

Source: Social Security Administration.

APPENDIX 15:
TABLE OF NUMBER OF SSI BENEFICIARIES
AND PAYMENTS DISTRIBUTED
(1974-1997)

YEAR	NUMBER OF SSI BENEFICIARIES	AMOUNTS PAID
1974	3,249,000	$5,096,000,000
1975	4,360,000	$5,716,000,000
1980	4,194,000	$7,714,000,000
1985	4,200,000	$10,749,000,000
1990	4,888,000	$16,132,000,000
1995	6,514,000	$27,037,000,000
1996	6,613,000	$26,501,000,000
1997	6,495,000	$26,675,000,000

Source: Social Security Administration.

APPENDIX 16:
NUMBER OF SUPPLEMENTAL SECURITY
INCOME RECIPIENTS (APRIL 2004)

AGE	NUMBER (thousands)	PERCENT	TOTAL PAYMENTS (millions of dollars)	AVERAGE MONTHLY PAYMENT
All recipients	6,950	100.0	$3,158	$427.10
Under 18	968	13.9	$525	$513.20
18 - 64	3,990	57.4	$1,933	$445.00
65 or older	1,992	28.7	$699	$349.60

Source: Social Security Administration.

APPENDIX 17:
MEDICARE PATIENTS' STATEMENT
OF RIGHTS

As a Medicare beneficiary, you have certain guaranteed rights. These rights protect you when you get health care; they assure you access to needed health care services; and they protect you against unethical practices. You have these Medicare rights whether you are in the Original Medicare Plan or another Medicare health plan. Your rights include:

1. The right to protection from discrimination in marketing and enrollment practices.

2. The right to information about what is covered and how much you have to pay.

3. The right to information about all treatment options available to you. You have the right to information about all your health care treatment options from your health care provider. Medicare forbids its health plans from making any rules that would stop a doctor from telling you everything you need to know about your health care, including treatment options. If you think your Medicare health plan may have kept your health care provider from telling you everything you need to know about your health care treatment options, you have a right to appeal.

4. The right to receive emergency care. If you have severe pain, an injury, sudden illness, or a suddenly worsening illness that you believe may cause your health serious danger without immediate care, you have the right to receive emergency care. You never need prior approval for emergency care, and you may receive emergency care anywhere in the United States.

5. The right to appeal decisions to deny or limit payment for medical care. If you are in the Original Medicare Plan, you have the right to appeal a denial of payment for a service you have been provided. Likewise, if you are enrolled in one of the other Medicare health

plans, you have the right to appeal the plan's denial for a service to be provided. As a Medicare beneficiary, you always have the right to appeal these decisions.

6. The right to know how your Medicare health plan pays its doctors. If you request information on how a Medicare health plan pays its doctors, the plan must give it to you in writing. You also have the right to know whether your doctor has a financial interest in a health care facility, such as a laboratory, since it could affect the medical advice he or she gives you.

7. The right to choose a women's health specialist.

8. The right, if you have a complex or serious medical condition, to receive a treatment plan that includes direct access to a specialist.

If you believe that any of your rights have been violated, please call the State Health Insurance Assistance Program in your State.

Source: Social Security Administration.

APPENDIX 18:
DIRECTORY OF STATE HEALTH INSURANCE ASSISTANCE PROGRAMS

STATE	TELEPHONE NUMBER
Alabama	1-800-243-5463
Alaska	1-800-478-6065
American Samoa	1-808-586-7299
Arizona	1-800-432-4040
Arkansas	1-800-852-5494
California	1-800-434-0222
Colorado	1-800-544-9181
Connecticut	1-800-994-9422
Delaware	1-800-336-9500
District of Columbia	1-800-336-9500
Florida	1-800-963-5337
Georgia	1-800-669-8387
Guam	1-808-586-7299
Hawaii	1-808-586-7299
Idaho	1-800-247-4422
Illinois	1-800-548-9034
Indiana	1-800-452-4800
Iowa	1-800-351-4664
Kansas	1-800-860-5260
Kentucky	1-800-372-2973
Louisiana	1-800-259-5301
Maine	1-800-750-5353
Maryland	1-800-243-3425

STATE	TELEPHONE NUMBER
Massachusetts	1-800-882-2003
Michigan	1-800-803-7174
Minnesota	1-800-333-2433
Mississippi	1-800-948-3090
Missouri	1-800-390-3330
Montana	1-800-332-2272
Nebraska	1-402-471-2201
Nevada	1-800-307-4444
New Hampshire	1-800-852-3388
New Jersey	1-800-792-8820
New Mexico	1-800-432-2080
New York	1-800-333-4114
North Carolina	1-800-443-9354
North Dakota	1-800-247-0560
Northern Mariana Islands	1-808-586-7299
Ohio	1-800-686-1578
Oklahoma	1-800-763-2828
Oregon	1-800-772-4134
Pennsylvania	1-800-783-7067
Puerto Rico	1-800-981-4355
Rhode Island	1-800-322-2880
South Carolina	1-800-868-9095
South Dakota	1-800-822-8804
Tennessee	1-800-525-2816
Texas	1-800-252-9240
Utah	1-800-439-3805
Vermont	1-800-642-5119
Virginia	1-800-522-3402
Virgin Islands	1-809-778-6311
Washington	1-800-397-4422
West Virginia	1-800-642-9004
Wisconsin	1-800-242-1060
Wyoming	1-800-586-4398

Source: Social Security Administration.

APPENDIX 19:
DIRECTORY OF STATE AGENCIES ON AGING

STATE	REGION	AGENCY	ADDRESS	TELEPHONE	FAX	E-MAIL
Alabama	Region IV	Alabama Department of Senior Services	770 Washington Avenue, Montgomery, AL 36130-1851	(334) 242-5743	(334) 242-5594	N/A
Alaska	Region X	Alaska Commission on Aging	P.O. Box 110209, Juneau, AK 99811-0209	(907) 465-3250	(907) 465-4716	acoa@admin.state.ak.us
Arizona	Region IX	Aging and Adult Administration	1789 West Jefferson Street, Phoenix, AZ 85007	(602) 542-4446	(602) 542-6575	N/A
Arkansas	Region VI	Division Aging and Adult Services	1417 Donaghey Plaza South, Little Rock, AR 72203-1437	(501) 682-2441	(501) 682-8155	ron.tatus@mail.state.ar.us

STATE	REGION	AGENCY	ADDRESS	TELEPHONE	FAX	E-MAIL
California	Region IX	California Department of Aging	1600 K Street, Sacramento, CA 95814	(916) 322-5290	(916) 324-1903	lterry@aging.state.ca.us
Colorado	Region VIII	Aging and Adult Services	1575 Sherman Street, Denver, CO 80203	(303) 866-2800	(303) 866-2696	viola.mcneace@state.co.us
Connecticut	Region I	Division of Elderly Services	25 Sigourney Street, Hartford, CT 06106-5033	(860) 424-5298	(860) 424-4966	adultserv.dss@po.state.ct.us
Delaware	Region III	Delaware Division of Services for Aging	1901 North DuPont Highway, New Castle, DE 19720	(302) 577-4791	(302) 577-4793	dsaapdinfo@state.de.us
Florida	Region IV	Department of Elder Affairs	4040 Esplanade Way, Tallahassee, FL 32399-7000	(850) 414-2000	(850) 414-2004	information@elderaffairs.org
Georgia	Region IV	Division of Aging Services	2 Peachtree Street N.E., Atlanta, GA 30303-3142	(404) 657-5258	(404) 657-5285	dhrconstituentservices@dhr.state.ga.us
Hawaii	Region IX	Hawaii Executive Office on Aging	250 South Hotel Street, Honolulu, HI 96813-2831	(808) 586-0100	(808) 586-0185	eoa@mail.health.state.hi.us

STATE	REGION	AGENCY	ADDRESS	TELEPHONE	FAX	E-MAIL
Idaho	Region X	Idaho Commission on Aging	P.O. Box 83720, Boise, ID 83720-0007	(208) 334-3833	(208) 334-3033	N/A
Illinois	Region V	Illinois Department on Aging	421 East Capitol Avenue, Springfield, IL 62701-1789	(217) 785-3356	(217) 785-4477	ilsenior@aging.state.il.us
Indiana	Region V	Bureau of Aging and In-Home Services	402 W. Washington Street, P.O. Box 7083, Indianapolis, IN 46207-7083	(317) 232-7020	(317) 232-7867	jlmiller@fssa.state.in.us
Iowa	Region VII	Iowa Department of Elder Affairs	200 Tenth Street, Des Moines, IA 50309-3609	(515) 242-3333	(515) 242-3300	sherry.james@dea.state.ia.us
Kansas	Region VII	Department on Aging	503 S. Kansas Ave., Topeka, KS 66603-3404	(785) 296-4986	(785) 296-0256	E-mail: wwwmail@aging.state.ks.us
Kentucky	Region IV	Office of Aging Services	275 East Main Street, Frankfort, KY 40621	(502) 564-6930	(502) 564-4595	N/A
Louisiana	Region VI	Governor's Office of Elderly Affairs	P.O. Box 80374, Baton Rouge, LA 70898-0374	(225) 342-7100	(225) 342-7133	PFARceneaux@goea.state.la.us

STATE	REGION	AGENCY	ADDRESS	TELEPHONE	FAX	E-MAIL
Maine	Region I	Bureau of Elder and Adult Services	35 Anthony Avenue, Augusta, ME 04333	(207) 624-5335	(207) 624-5361	webmaster_beas@state.me.us
Maryland	Region III	Maryland Department of Aging	301 West Preston Street, Baltimore, MD 21201-2374	(410) 767-1100	(410) 333-7943	ptc@mail.ooa.state.md.us
Massachusetts	Region I	Massachusetts Executive Office of Elder Affairs	One Ashburton Place, Boston, MA 02108	(617) 727-7750	(617) 727-9368	www.state.ma.us/elder
Michigan	Region V	Michigan Office of Services to the Aging	611 W. Ottawa, N. Ottawa Tower, P.O. Box 30676, Lansing, MI 48909	(517) 373-8230	(517) 373-4092	N/A
Minnesota	Region V	Minnesota Board on Aging	444 Lafayette Road, St. Paul, MN 55155-3843	(651) 296-2770	(651) 297-7855	N/A
Missouri	Region VII	Division of Senior Services	615 Howerton Court, Jefferson City, MO 65102-1337	(573) 751-3082	(573) 751-8687	pwoodsma@mail.state.mo.us
Montana	Region VIII	Senior and Long Term Care Division	P.O. Box 4210, Helena, MT 59620	(406) 444-4077	(406) 444-7743	N/A

STATE	REGION	AGENCY	ADDRESS	TELEPHONE	FAX	E-MAIL
Nebraska	Region VII	Division on Aging	1343 M Street, Lincoln, NE 68509-5044	(402) 471-2307	(402) 471-4619	mark.intermill@hhs.state.ne.us
Nevada	Region IX	Nevada Division for Aging Services	3416 Goni Road, Carson City, NV 89706	(775) 687-4210	(775) 687-4264	dascc@govmail.state.nv.us
New Hampshire	Region I	Division of Elderly and Adult Services	129 Pleasant Street, Concord, NH 03301	(603) 271-4680	(603) 271-4643	N/A
New Jersey	Region II	New Jersey Division of Senior Affairs	P.O Box 807, Trenton, NJ 08625-0807	(609) 943-3436	(609) 588-3317	seniors@doh.state.nj.us
New Mexico	Region VI	New Mexico Office of Aging	228 East Palace Avenue, Santa Fe, NM 87501	(505) 827-7640	(505) 827-7649	nmaoa@state.nm.us
New York	Region II	New York State Office for The Aging	2 Empire State Plaza, Albany, NY 12223-1251	(518) 474-5731	(518) 474-0608	nysofa@ofa.state.ny.us
North Carolina	Region IV	Division of Aging	2101 Mail Service Center, Raleigh, NC 27699-2101	(919) 733-3983	(919) 733-0443	mary.beth@ncmail.net
North Dakota	Region VIII	Aging Services Division	600 South 2nd Street, Bismarck, ND 58504	(701) 328-891	(800) 451-8693 (701) 328-8989	dhssrinf@state.nd.us

STATE	REGION	AGENCY	ADDRESS	TELEPHONE	FAX	E-MAIL
Ohio	Region V	Ohio Department of Aging	50 West Broad Street, Columbus, OH 43215-5928	(614) 466-5500	(614) 466-5741	N/A
Oklahoma	Region VI	Aging Services Division	312 N.E. 28th Street, Oklahoma City, OK 73125	(405) 521-2281	(405) 521-2086	Cynthia.Kinkade@okdhs.org
Oregon	Region X	Seniors and People with Disabilities	500 Summer Street N.E., Salem, OR 97301-1073	(503) 945-5811	(503) 373-7823	sdsd.info@state.or.us
Pennsylvania	Region III	Pennsylvania Department of Aging	555 Walnut Street, Harrisburg, PA 17101-1919	(717) 783-1550	(717) 772-3382	aging@state.pa.us
Rhode Island	Region I	Department of Elderly Affairs	160 Pine Street, Providence, RI 02903-3708	(401) 222-2858	(401) 222-2130	larry@dea.state.ri.us
South Carolina	Region IV	Office of Senior and Long Term Care Services	P.O. Box 8206, Columbia, SC 29202-8206	(803) 898-2501	(803) 898-4515	N/A
South Dakota	Region VIII	Office of Adult Services and Aging	700 Governors Drive, Pierre, SD 57501-2291	(605) 773-3656	(605) 773-6834	asaging@dss.state.sd.us

STATE	REGION	AGENCY	ADDRESS	TELEPHONE	FAX	E-MAIL
Tennessee	Region IV	Commission on Aging and Disability	500 Deaderick Street, Nashville, Tennessee 37243-0860	(615) 741-2056	(615) 741-3309	N/A
Texas	Region VI	Texas Department on Aging	4900 North Lamar, Austin, TX 78751-2316	(512) 424-6840	(512) 424-6890	mail@tdoa.state.tx.us
Utah	Region VIII	Division of Aging and Adult Services	120 North 200 West, Salt Lake City, UT 84145-0500	(801) 538-3910	(801) 538-4395	DAAS@hs.state.ut.us
Vermont	Region I	Vermont Department of Aging and Disabilities	103 South Main Street, Waterbury, VT 05671-2301	(802) 241-2400	(802) 241-2325	patrick@dad.state.vt.us
Virginia	Region III	Virginia Department for the Aging	1600 Forest Avenue, Richmond, VA 23229	(804) 662-9333	(804) 662-9354	aging@vdh.state.va.us
Washington	Region X	Aging and Adult Services Administration	P.O. Box 45050, Olympia, WA 98504-5050	(360) 725-2310	(360) 438-8633	askdshs@dshs.wa.gov
West Virginia	Region III	West Virginia Bureau of Senior Services	1900 Kanawha Boulevard East, Charleston, WV 25305	(304) 558-3317	(304) 558-5699	info@boss.state.wv.us

STATE	REGION	AGENCY	ADDRESS	TELEPHONE	FAX	E-MAIL
Wisconsin	Region V	Bureau of Aging and Long Term Care Resources	1 West Wilson Street, Madison, WI 53707-7850	(608) 266-2536	(608) 267-3203	snittma@dhfs.state.wi.us
Wyoming	Region VIII	Division on Aging	6101 Yellowstone Road, Cheyenne, WY 82002-0710	(307) 777-7986	(307) 777-5340	wyaging@state.wy.us

APPENDIX 20:
DIRECTORY OF NATIONAL ORGANIZATIONS FOR THE ELDERLY

AGENCY	WEBSITE	FUNCTION
Administration on Aging	http://www.aoa.gov	Federal government agency that provides information to older persons and their families on age-related issues
Alzheimer's Association	http://www.alz.org	Provides information for families looking for residential care for someone with Alzheimer's disease
American Association of Homes and Services for the Aging	http://www.aahsa.org/public/consumer.htm	National organization consisting of more than 5,000 not-for-profit nursing homes, continuing care retirement communities, senior housing and assisted living facilities, and community services for the elderly

AGENCY	WEBSITE	FUNCTION
American Association of Retired Persons	http://www.aarp.org	A non-profit, non-partisan association dedicated to shaping and enriching the American aging experience
American Geriatrics Society	http://www.americangeriatrics.org	A professional organization of health-care providers dedicated to improving the health and well-being of older people and effecting change in the provision of health care to older Americans
Association for the Protection of the Elderly	http://www.apeape.org	An association dedicated to improving nursing home conditions and educating nursing home residents and their families on quality of care issues
The Centers for Medicare and Medicaid Services	http://www.medicare.gov/nhcompare/home.asp	Federal agency that oversees Medicare and Medicaid and has a web site to help people in their search for a nursing home
Elder Abuse Prevention Information, Resource Guide	http://www.oaktrees.org/elder	Organization dedicated to stopping the abuse of the elderly
Eldercare Locator	http://www.aoa.dhhs.gov/elderpage/locator.html	Nationwide directory assistance service designed to help older persons and caregivers locate local support resources for aging Americans
The National Center for Elder Abuse	http://www.elderabusecenter.org	Federal grant-funded partnership of leading organizations involved with preventing elder abuse

AGENCY	WEBSITE	FUNCTION
National Citizens' Coalition for Nursing Home Reform	http://www.nccnhr.org	Provides information on choosing a nursing home and other information for families who want quality nursing home care
National Health Law Program	http://www.healthlaw.org	A national public interest law firm seeking to improve health care for America's elderly, poor, disabled, and minority citizens
National Institute on Aging	http://www.nia.nih.gov	Federal agency of the National Institutes of Health that promotes healthy aging by supporting and conducting research and public education on aging issues
National Senior Citizen Law Center	http://www.nsclc.org	National advocates devoted to promoting the independence and well-being of elderly and disabled people
Nursing Home Info	http://www.nursinghomeinfo.com	Financial and Internet marketing consulting firm specializing in the senior care area which provides nationwide nursing home information
United States Department of Health and Human Services	http://aspe.os.dhhs.gov	Website devoted to Medicare issues

APPENDIX 21:
APPOINTMENT OF REPRESENTATIVE

Social Security Administration
Please read the back of the last copy before you complete this form.

Form Approved
OMB No. 0960-0527

Name (Claimant) (Print or Type)	Social Security Number
Wage Earner (If Different)	Social Security Number

Part I   APPOINTMENT OF REPRESENTATIVE

I appoint this person, _____ ,
                                       (Name and Address)

to act as my representative in connection with my claim(s) or asserted right(s) under:

☐ Title II   ☐ Title XVI   ☐ Title IV FMSHA   ☐ Title XVIII   ☐ Title VIII
(RSDI)   (SSI)   (Black Lung)   (Medicare Coverage)   (SVB)

This person may, entirely in my place, make any request or give any notice; give or draw out evidence or information; get information; and receive any notice in connection with my pending claim(s) or asserted right(s).

☐   I am appointing, or I now have, more than one representative. My main representative
is _____ .
                  (Name of Principal Representative)

Signature (Claimant)	Address	
Telephone Number (with Area Code)	Fax Number (with Area Code)	Date

Part II   ACCEPTANCE OF APPOINTMENT

I, _____ , hereby accept the above appointment. I certify that I have not been suspended or prohibited from practice before the Social Security Administration; that I am not disqualified from representing the claimant as a current or former officer or employee of the United States; and that I will not charge or collect any fee for the representation, even if a third party will pay the fee, unless it has been approved in accordance with the laws and rules referred to on the reverse side of the representative's copy of this form. If I decide not to charge or collect a fee for the representation, I will notify the Social Security Administration. (Completion of Part III satisfies this requirement.)

☐ I am an attorney.   ☐ I am not an attorney.   (Check one.)

I declare under penalty of perjury that I have examined all the information on this form, and on any accompanying statements or forms, and it is true and correct to the best of my knowledge.

Signature (Representative)	Address	
Telephone Number (with Area Code)	Fax Number (with Area Code)	Date

Part III (Optional)   WAIVER OF FEE

I waive my right to charge and collect a fee under sections 206 and 1631(d)(2) of the Social Security Act. I release my client (the claimant) from any obligations, contractual or otherwise, which may be owed to me for services I have provided in connection with my client's claim(s) or asserted right(s).

Signature (Representative)	Date

Part IV (Optional)   ATTORNEY'S WAIVER OF DIRECT PAYMENT

I waive only my right to direct payment of a fee from the withheld past-due retirement, survivors, disability insurance or black lung benefits of my client (the claimant). I do not waive my right to request fee approval and to collect a fee directly from my client or a third party.

Signature (Attorney Representative)	Date

Form SSA-1696-U4 (5-2003) EF (5-2003)   (See Important Information on Reverse)   FILE COPY
Destroy Prior Editions

INFORMATION FOR CLAIMANTS

What A Representative May Do

We will work directly with your appointed representative unless he or she asks us to work directly with you. Your representative may:

o get information from your claim(s) file;
o give us evidence or information to support your claim;
o come with you, or for you, to any interview, conference, or hearing you have with us;
o request a reconsideration, hearing, or Appeals Council review; and
o help you and your witnesses prepare for a hearing and question any witnesses.

Also, your representative will receive a copy of the decision(s) we make on your claim(s). We will rely on your representative to tell you about the status of your claim(s), but you still may call or visit us for information.

You and your representative(s) are responsible for giving Social Security accurate information. It is wrong to knowingly and willingly furnish false information. Doing so may result in criminal prosecution.

We usually continue to work with your representative until (1) you tell us that he or she no longer represents you; or (2) your representative tells us that he or she is withdrawing or indicates that his or her services have ended (for example, by filing a fee petition or not pursuing an appeal). We do not continue to work with someone who is suspended or disqualified from representing claimants.

What Your Representative(s) May Charge

Each representative you appoint can ask for a fee. To charge you a fee for services, your representative must get our approval. (Even when someone else will pay the fee for you, for example, an insurance company, your representative usually must get our approval.) One way is to file a fee petition. The other way is to file a fee agreement with us. In either case, your representative cannot charge you more than the fee amount we approve. If he or she does, promptly report this to your Social Security office.

o Filing A Fee Petition

Your representative may ask for approval of a fee by giving us a fee petition when his or her work on your claim(s) is complete. This written request describes in detail the amount of time he or she spent on each service provided you. The request also gives the amount of the fee the representative wants to charge for these services. Your representative must give you a copy of the fee petition and each attachment. If you disagree with the information shown in the fee petition, contact your Social Security office. Please do this within 20 days of receiving your copy of the petition.

We will review the petition and consider the reasonable value of the services provided. Then we will tell you in writing the amount of the fee we approve.

Form SSA-1696-U4 (5-2003) EF (5-2003)

What Your Representative(s) May Charge, continued

o Filing A Fee Agreement

If you and your representative have a written fee agreement, one of you must give it to us before we decide your claim(s). We usually will approve the agreement if you both signed it; the fee you agreed on is no more than 25 percent of past-due benefits, or $5,300 (or a higher amount we set and announced in the Federal Register), whichever is less; we approve your claim(s); and your claim results in past-due benefits. We will tell you in writing the amount of the fee your representative can charge based on the agreement.

If we do not approve the fee agreement, we will tell you and your representative in writing. Then your representative must file a fee petition to charge and collect a fee.

After we tell you the amount of the fee your representative can charge, you or your representative can ask us to look at it again if either or both of you disagree with the amount. (If we approved a fee agreement, the person who decided your claim(s) also may ask us to lower the amount.) Someone who did not decide the amount of the fee the first time will review and finally decide the amount of the fee.

How Much You Pay

You never owe more than the fee we approve, except for:

o any fee a Federal court allows for your representative's services before it; and
o out-of-pocket expenses your representative incurs or expects to incur, for example, the cost of getting your doctor's or hospital records. Our approval is not needed for such expenses.

Your representative may accept money in advance as long as he or she holds it in a trust or escrow account. If an attorney represents you and your retirement, survivors, disability insurance, or black lung claim results in past-due benefits, we usually withhold 25 percent of your past-due benefits to pay toward the fee for you.

You must pay your representative directly:

o the rest of the fee you owe
  - if the amount of the fee is more than any amount(s) your representative held for you in a trust or escrow account and we withheld and paid your attorney for you.
o all of the fee you owe
  - if we did not withhold past-due benefits, for example, when your representative is not an attorney or the benefits are supplemental security income; or
  - if we withheld, but later paid you the money because your attorney did not either ask for our approval until after 60 days of the date of your notice of award or tell us on time that he or she planned to ask for a fee.

APPOINTMENT OF REPRESENTATIVE

Social Security Administration

Please read the back of the last copy before you complete this form.

Form Approved
OMB No. 0960-0527

Name (Claimant) (Print or Type)	Social Security Number

Wage Earner (If Different)	Social Security Number

Part I   **APPOINTMENT OF REPRESENTATIVE**

I appoint this person, _____ ,
(Name and Address)

to act as my representative in connection with my claim(s) or asserted right(s) under:

☐ Title II (RSDI)   ☐ Title XVI (SSI)   ☐ Title IV FMSHA (Black Lung)   ☐ Title XVIII (Medicare Coverage)   ☐ Title VIII (SVB)

This person may, entirely in my place, make any request or give any notice; give or draw out evidence or information; get information; and receive any notice in connection with my pending claim(s) or asserted right(s).

☐ I am appointing, or I now have, more than one representative. My main representative is _____
(Name of Principal Representative)

Signature (Claimant)	Address

Telephone Number (with Area Code)	Fax Number (with Area Code)	Date

Part II   **ACCEPTANCE OF APPOINTMENT**

I, _____ , hereby accept the above appointment. I certify that I have not been suspended or prohibited from practice before the Social Security Administration; that I am not disqualified from representing the claimant as a current or former officer or employee of the United States; and that I will not charge or collect any fee for the representation, even if a third party will pay the fee, unless it has been approved in accordance with the laws and rules referred to on the reverse side of the representative's copy of this form. If I decide not to charge or collect a fee for the representation, I will notify the Social Security Administration. (Completion of Part III satisfies this requirement.)

☐ I am an attorney.   ☐ I am not an attorney.   (Check one.)

I declare under penalty of perjury that I have examined all the information on this form, and on any accompanying statements or forms, and it is true and correct to the best of my knowledge.

Signature (Representative)	Address

Telephone Number (with Area Code)	Fax Number (with Area Code)	Date

Part III (Optional)   **WAIVER OF FEE**

I waive my right to charge and collect a fee under sections 206 and 1631(d)(2) of the Social Security Act. I release my client (the claimant) from any obligations, contractual or otherwise, which may be owed to me for services I have provided in connection with my client's claim(s) or asserted right(s).

Signature (Representative)	Date

Part IV (Optional)   **ATTORNEY'S WAIVER OF DIRECT PAYMENT**

I waive only my right to direct payment of a fee from the withheld past-due retirement, survivors, disability insurance or black lung benefits of my client (the claimant). I do not waive my right to request fee approval and to collect a fee directly from my client or a third party.

Signature (Attorney Representative)	Date

Form SSA-1696-U4 (5-2003) EF (5-2003)   (See Important Information on Reverse)   CLAIMANT'S COPY
Destroy Prior Editions

Social Security Law   163

INFORMATION FOR CLAIMANTS

What A Representative May Do

We will work directly with your appointed representative unless he or she asks us to work directly with you. Your representative may:

o get information from your claim(s) file;
o give us evidence or information to support your claim;
o come with you, or for you, to any interview, conference, or hearing you have with us;
o request a reconsideration, hearing, or Appeals Council review; and
o help you and your witnesses prepare for a hearing and question any witnesses.

Also, your representative will receive a copy of the decision(s) we make on your claim(s). We will rely on your representative to tell you about the status of your claim(s), but you still may call or visit us for information.

You and your representative(s) are responsible for giving Social Security accurate information. It is wrong to knowingly and willingly furnish false information. Doing so may result in criminal prosecution.

We usually continue to work with your representative until (1) you tell us that he or she no longer represents you; or (2) your representative tells us that he or she is withdrawing or indicates that his or her services have ended (for example, by filing a fee petition or not pursuing an appeal). We do not continue to work with someone who is suspended or disqualified from representing claimants.

What Your Representative(s) May Charge

Each representative you appoint can ask for a fee. To charge you a fee for services, your representative must get our approval. (Even when someone else will pay the fee for you, for example, an insurance company, your representative usually must get our approval.) One way is to file a fee petition. The other way is to file a fee agreement with us. In either case, your representative cannot charge you more than the fee amount we approve. If he or she does, promptly report this to your Social Security office.

o Filing A Fee Petition

Your representative may ask for approval of a fee by giving us a fee petition when his or her work on your claim(s) is complete. This written request describes in detail the amount of time he or she spent on each service provided you. The request also gives the amount of the fee the representative wants to charge for these services. Your representative must give you a copy of the fee petition and each attachment. If you disagree with the information shown in the fee petition, contact your Social Security office. Please do this within 20 days of receiving your copy of the petition.

We will review the petition and consider the reasonable value of the services provided. Then we will tell you in writing the amount of the fee we approve.

Form SSA-1696-U4 (5-2003) EF (5-2003)

What Your Representative(s) May Charge, continued

o Filing A Fee Agreement

If you and your representative have a written fee agreement, one of you must give it to us before we decide your claim(s). We usually will approve the agreement if you both signed it; the fee you agreed on is no more than 25 percent of past-due benefits, or $5,300 (or a higher amount we set and announce in the Federal Register), whichever is less; we approve your claim(s); and your claim results in past-due benefits. We will tell you in writing the amount of the fee your representative can charge based on the agreement.

If we do not approve the fee agreement, we will tell you and your representative in writing. Then your representative must file a fee petition to charge and collect a fee.

After we tell you the amount of the fee your representative can charge, you or your representative can ask us to look at it again if either or both of you disagree with the amount. (If we approved a fee agreement, the person who decided your claim(s) also may ask us to lower the amount.) Someone who did not decide the amount of the fee the first time will review and finally decide the amount of the fee.

How Much You Pay

You never owe more than the fee we approve, except for:

o any fee a Federal court allows for your representative's services before it; and
o out-of-pocket expenses your representative incurs or expects to incur, for example, the cost of getting your doctor's or hospital records. Our approval is not needed for such expenses.

Your representative may accept money in advance as long as he or she holds it in a trust or escrow account. If an attorney represents you and your retirement, survivors, disability insurance, or black lung claim results in past-due benefits, we usually withhold 25 percent of your past-due benefits to pay toward the fee for you.

You must pay your representative directly:

o the rest of the fee you owe

- if the amount of the fee is more than any amount(s) your representative held for you in a trust or escrow account and we withheld and paid your attorney for you.

o all of the fee you owe

- if we did not withhold past-due benefits, for example, when your representative is not an attorney or the benefits are supplemental security income; or

- if we withheld, but later paid you the money because your attorney did not either ask for our approval until after 60 days of the date of your notice of award or tell us on time that he or she planned to ask for a fee.

Social Security Administration
Please read the back of the last copy before you complete this form.

Form Approved
OMB No. 0960-0527

Name (Claimant) (Print or Type)	Social Security Number
Wage Earner (If Different)	Social Security Number

Part I   APPOINTMENT OF REPRESENTATIVE

I appoint this person, _____ ,
                                                   (Name and Address)

to act as my representative in connection with my claim(s) or asserted right(s) under:

☐ Title II (RSDI)   ☐ Title XVI (SSI)   ☐ Title IV FMSHA (Black Lung)   ☐ Title XVIII (Medicare Coverage)   ☐ Title VIII (SVB)

This person may, entirely in my place, make any request or give any notice; give or draw out evidence or information; get information; and receive any notice in connection with my pending claim(s) or asserted right(s).

☐   I am appointing, or I now have, more than one representative. My main representative is _____ .
                       (Name of Principal Representative)

Signature (Claimant)	Address	
Telephone Number (with Area Code)	Fax Number (with Area Code)	Date

Part II   ACCEPTANCE OF APPOINTMENT

I, _____ , hereby accept the above appointment. I certify that I have not been suspended or prohibited from practice before the Social Security Administration; that I am not disqualified from representing the claimant as a current or former officer or employee of the United States; and that I will not charge or collect any fee for the representation, even if a third party will pay the fee, unless it has been approved in accordance with the laws and rules referred to on the reverse side of the representative's copy of this form. If I decide not to charge or collect a fee for the representation, I will notify the Social Security Administration. (Completion of Part III satisfies this requirement.)

☐ I am an attorney.   ☐ I am not an attorney.   (Check one.)

I declare under penalty of perjury that I have examined all the information on this form, and on any accompanying statements or forms, and it is true and correct to the best of my knowledge.

Signature (Representative)	Address	
Telephone Number (with Area Code)	Fax Number (with Area Code)	Date

Part III (Optional)   WAIVER OF FEE

I waive my right to charge and collect a fee under sections 206 and 1631(d)(2) of the Social Security Act. I release my client (the claimant) from any obligations, contractual or otherwise, which may be owed to me for services I have provided in connection with my client's claim(s) or asserted right(s).

Signature (Representative)	Date

Part IV (Optional)   ATTORNEY'S WAIVER OF DIRECT PAYMENT

I waive only my right to direct payment of a fee from the withheld past-due retirement, survivors, disability insurance or black lung benefits of my client (the claimant). I do not waive my right to request fee approval and to collect a fee directly from my client or a third party.

Signature (Attorney Representative)	Date

Form SSA-1696-U4 (5-2003) EF (5-2003)   (See Important Information on Reverse)   REPRESENTATIVE'S COPY
Destroy Prior Editions

INFORMATION FOR REPRESENTATIVES

Fees For Representation

An attorney or other person who wants to charge or collect a fee for providing services in connection with a claim before the Social Security Administration must first obtain our approval of the fee for representation. The only exceptions are if the fee is for services provided:

o   when a nonprofit organization or government agency will pay the fee and any expenses from government funds and the claimant incurs no liability, directly or indirectly, for the cost(s);

o   in an official capacity such as legal guardian, committee, or similar court-appointed office and the court has approved the fee in question; or

o   in representing the claimant before a court of law. A representative who has provided services in a claim before both the Social Security Administration and a court of law may seek a fee from either or both, but neither tribunal has the authority to set a fee for the other.

Obtaining Approval Of A Fee

To charge a fee for services, you must use one of two, mutually exclusive fee approval processes. You must file either a fee petition or a fee agreement with us. In either case, you cannot charge more than the fee amount we approve.

o   Fee Petition Process

You may ask for approval of a fee by giving us a fee petition when you have completed your services to the claimant. This written request must describe in detail the amount of time you spent on each service provided and the amount of the fee you are requesting.

You must give the claimant a copy of the fee petition and each attachment. The claimant may disagree with the information shown by contacting a Social Security office within 20 days of receiving his or her copy of the fee petition. We will consider the reasonable value of the services provided, and send you notice of the amount of the fee you can charge.

o   Fee Agreement Process

If you and the claimant have a written fee agreement, either of you must give it to us before we decide the claim(s). We usually will approve the agreement if you both signed it; the fee you agreed on is no more than 25 percent of past-due benefits, or $5,300 (or a higher amount we set and announce in the Federal Register), whichever is less; we approve the claim(s); and the claim results in past-due benefits. We will send you a copy of the notice we send the claimant telling him or her the amount of the fee you can charge based on the agreement.

If we do not approve the fee agreement, we will tell you in writing. We also will tell you and the claimant that you must file a fee petition if you wish to charge and collect a fee.

After we tell you the amount of the fee you can charge, you or the claimant may ask us in writing to review the approved fee. (If we approved a fee agreement, the person who decided the claim(s) also may ask us to lower the amount.) Someone who did not decide the amount of the fee the first time will review and finally decide the amount of the fee.

Form SSA-1696-U4 (5-2003) EF (5-2003)

Collecting A Fee

You may accept money in advance, as long as you hold it in a trust or escrow account. The claimant never owes you more than the fee we approve, except for:

o   any fee a Federal court allows for your services before it; and

o   out-of-pocket expenses you incur or expect to incur, for example, the cost of getting evidence. Our approval is not needed for such expenses.

If you are not an attorney, you must collect the approved fee from the claimant.

If you are an attorney, we usually withhold 25 percent of any past-due benefits that result from a favorably decided retirement, survivors, disability insurance, or black lung claim. Once we approve a fee, we pay you all or part of the fee from the funds withheld. We will also charge you the assessment required by section 206(d) of the Social Security Act. You cannot charge or collect this expense from the claimant. You must collect from the claimant:

o   the rest he or she owes
  -   if the amount of the fee is more than the amount of money we withheld and paid you for the claimant, and any amount you held for the claimant in a trust or escrow account.

o   all of the fee he or she owes
  -   if we did not withhold past-due benefits, for example, because the benefits are supplemental security income or there are no past-due benefits; or if we withheld, but later paid the money to the claimant because you did not either ask for our approval until after 60 days of the date of the notice of award or tell us on time that you planned to ask for a fee.

Conflict Of Interest And Penalties

For improper acts, you can be suspended or disqualified from representing anyone before the Social Security Administration. You also can face criminal prosecution. Improper acts include:

o   If you are or were an officer or employee of the United States, providing services as a representative in certain claims against and other matters affecting the Federal government.

o   Knowingly and willingly furnishing false information.

o   Charging or collecting an unauthorized fee or too much for services provided in any claim, including services before a court which made a favorable decision.

References

o   18 U.S.C. §§ 203, 205, and 207; 30 U.S.C. § 923(b); and 42 U.S.C. §§ 406(a), 1320a-6, and 1383(d)(2)

o   20 CFR §§ 404.1700 et. seq., 410.684 et. seq., and 416.1500 et. seq.

o   Social Security Rulings 88-10c (C.E. 1988), 85-3 (C.E. 1985), 83-27 (C.E. 1983), and 82-39 (C.E. 1982)

Social Security Administration

Please read the back of the last copy before you complete this form.

Form Approved
OMB No. 0960-0527

Name (Claimant) (Print or Type)	Social Security Number

Wage Earner (If Different)	Social Security Number

Part I   APPOINTMENT OF REPRESENTATIVE

I appoint this person, _____
(Name and Address)

to act as my representative in connection with my claim(s) or asserted right(s) under:

☐ Title II (RSDI)   ☐ Title XVI (SSI)   ☐ Title IV FMSHA (Black Lung)   ☐ Title XVIII (Medicare Coverage)   ☐ Title VIII (SVB)

This person may, entirely in my place, make any request or give any notice; give or draw out evidence or information; get information; and receive any notice in connection with my pending claim(s) or asserted right(s).

☐   I am appointing, or I now have, more than one representative. My main representative is _____ .
(Name of Principal Representative)

Signature (Claimant)	Address

Telephone Number (with Area Code)	Fax Number (with Area Code)	Date

Part II   ACCEPTANCE OF APPOINTMENT

I, _____ , hereby accept the above appointment. I certify that I have not been suspended or prohibited from practice before the Social Security Administration; that I am not disqualified from representing the claimant as a current or former officer or employee of the United States; and that I will not charge or collect any fee for the representation, even if a third party will pay the fee, unless it has been approved in accordance with the laws and rules referred to on the reverse side of the representative's copy of this form. If I decide not to charge or collect a fee for the representation, I will notify the Social Security Administration. (Completion of Part III satisfies this requirement.)

☐ I am an attorney.   ☐ I am not an attorney.   (Check one.)

I declare under penalty of perjury that I have examined all the information on this form, and on any accompanying statements or forms, and it is true and correct to the best of my knowledge.

Signature (Representative)	Address

Telephone Number (with Area Code)	Fax Number (with Area Code)	Date

Part III (Optional)   WAIVER OF FEE

I waive my right to charge and collect a fee under sections 206 and 1631(d)(2) of the Social Security Act. I release my client (the claimant) from any obligations, contractual or otherwise, which may be owed to me for services I have provided in connection with my client's claim(s) or asserted right(s).

Signature (Representative)	Date

Part IV (Optional)   ATTORNEY'S WAIVER OF DIRECT PAYMENT

I waive only my right to direct payment of a fee from the withheld past-due retirement, survivors, disability insurance or black lung benefits of my client (the claimant). I do not waive my right to request fee approval and to collect a fee directly from my client or a third party.

Signature (Attorney Representative)	Date

Form SSA-1696-U4 (5-2003) EF (5-2003)   (See Important Information on Reverse)   OHA COPY
Destroy Prior Editions

APPOINTMENT OF REPRESENTATIVE

COMPLETING THIS FORM TO APPOINT A REPRESENTATIVE

Choosing To Be Represented

You can choose to have a representative help you when you do business with Social Security. We will work with your representative, just as we would with you. It is important that you select a qualified person because, once appointed, your representative may act for you in most Social Security matters. We give more information, and examples of what a representative may do, on the back of the "Claimant's Copy" of this form.

Paperwork and Privacy Act Notice

The Social Security Administration will recognize someone else as your representative if you sign a written notice appointing that person and, if he or she is not an attorney, that person signs the notice agreeing to be your representative. (You can read more about this in our regulations: 20 CFR §§ 404.1707, 410.684, and 416.1507.) Giving the information this form requests is voluntary. Without it though, we may not work with the person you choose to represent you.

How To Complete This Form

Please print or type. At the top, show your full name and your Social Security number. If your claim is based on another person's work and earnings, also show the "wage earner's" name and Social Security number. If you appoint more than one person, you may want to complete a form for each of them.

Part I Appointment of Representative

Give the name and address of the person(s) you are appointing. You may appoint an attorney or any other qualified person to represent you. You also may appoint more than one person, but see "What Your Representative(s) May Charge" on the back of the "Claimant's Copy" of this form. You can appoint one or more persons in a firm, corporation, or other organization as your representative(s), but you may not appoint a law firm, legal aid group, corporation, or organization itself.

Check the block(s) showing the program(s) under which you have a claim. You may check more than one block. Check:

o   Title II (RSDI), if your claim concerns retirement, survivors, or disability insurance benefits.

o   Title XVI (SSI), if your claim concerns supplemental security income.

o   Title IV FMSHA (Black Lung), if your claim concerns black lung benefits under the Federal Mine Safety and Health Act.

o   Title XVIII (Medicare Coverage), if your claim concerns entitlement to Medicare or enrollment in the Supplementary Medical Insurance (SMI) plan.

If you will have more than one representative, check the block and give the name of the person you want to be the main representative.

Form SSA-1696-U4 (5-2003) EF (5-2003)

How To Complete This Form, continued

Sign your name, but print or type your address, your area code and telephone number, and the date.

Part II Acceptance of Appointment

Each person you appoint (named in part I) completes this part, preferably in all cases. If the person is not an attorney, he or she must give his or her name, state that he or she accepts the appointment, and sign the form.

Part III (Optional) Waiver of Fee

Your representative may complete this part if he or she will not charge any fee for the services provided in this claim. If you appoint a second representative or co-counsel who also will not charge a fee, he or she also should sign this part or give us a separate, written waiver statement.

Part IV (Optional)   Attorney's Waiver of Direct Payment

Your representative may complete this part if he or she is an attorney who does not want direct payment of all or part of the approved fee from past-due retirement, survivors, disability insurance, or black lung benefits withheld.

Paperwork Reduction Act Statement - This information collection meets the requirements of 44 U.S.C. § 3507, as amended by Section 2 of the Paperwork Reduction Act of 1995. You do not need to answer these questions unless we display a valid Office of Management and Budget control number. We estimate that it will take about 10 minutes to read the instructions, gather the facts, and answer the questions. SEND THE COMPLETED FORM TO YOUR LOCAL SOCIAL SECURITY OFFICE. The office is listed under U. S. Government agencies in your telephone directory or you may call Social Security at 1-800-772-1213. *You may send comments on our time estimate above to: SSA, 1338 Annex Building, Baltimore, MD 21235-0001. Send only comments relating to our time estimate to this address, not the completed form.*

References

o   18 U.S.C. §§ 203, 205, and 207; 30 U.S.C. § 923(b); and 42 U.S.C. §§ 406(a), 1320a-6, and 1383(d)(2)

o   20 CFR §§ 404.1700 et. seq., 410.684 et. seq., and 416.1500 et. seq.

o   Social Security Rulings 88-10c (C.E. 1988), 85-3 (C.E. 1985), 83-27 (C.E. 1983), and 82-39 (C.E. 1982)

APPENDIX 22:
DIRECTORY OF NATIONAL LEGAL SERVICES FOR THE ELDERLY

NAME	ADDRESS	TELEPHONE NUMBER
American Bar Association Commission on Legal Problems of the Elderly	1800 M Street N.W., Suite 200, Washington, DC 20036	202-331-2297
Center for Social Gerentology	117 No. 1st Street, Suite 204, Ann Arbor, MI 48104	313-665-1126
Legal Counsel for the Elderly	601 E Street N.W., Washington, D.C. 20004	202-434-2170
Legal Services for the Elderly	132 W. 43rd Street, 3rd Floor, New York, NY 10036	212-595-1340
Medicare Beneficiaries Defense Fund	1460 Broadway, 8th Floor, New York, NY 10036	212-869-3850
National Academy of Elder Law Attorneys	1604 N. Country Club Road, Tucson, AZ 85716	520-881-4005
National Caucus and Center on Black Aged	1424 K Street, NW, Suite 500, Washington, DC 20005	202-637-8400
National Health Law Program	2639 S. La Cienega Blvd., Los Angeles, CA 90034	213-204-6010
National Health Law Program	2025 M Street N.W., Washington, DC 20036	202-887-5310
National Senior Citizens Law Center	1052 W. 6th Street, 7th Floor, Los Angeles, CA 90017	213-482-3550
National Senior Citizens Law Center	1101 14th Street N.W., Suite 400, Washington, DC 20005	202-887-5280

APPENDIX 23:
PETITION TO OBTAIN FEE APPROVAL

SOCIAL SECURITY ADMINISTRATION	TOE 850	Form Approved OMB No. 0960-0104
PETITION TO OBTAIN APPROVAL OF A FEE FOR REPRESENTING A CLAIMANT BEFORE THE SOCIAL SECURITY ADMINISTRATION		**IMPORTANT INFORMATION ON REVERSE SIDE**

PAPERWORK/PRIVACY ACT NOTICE: Your response to this request is voluntary, but the Social Security Administration may not approve any fee unless it receives the information this form requests. The Administration will use the information to determine a fair value for services you rendered to the claimant named below, as provided in section 206 of the Social Security Act (42 U.S.C. 406).

I request approval to charge a fee of ———————▶ | Fee $ _____ (Show the dollar amount)

for services performed as the representative of ———▶ | Mr.
Mrs.
Ms. _____

My Services Began: ____ / ____ / _____
Month   Day   Year

| Type(s) of claim(s)

My Services Ended: ____ / ____ / _____

Enter the name and the Social Security number of the person on whose Social Security record the claim is based
_____ / __ / _____

1.	Itemize on a separate page or pages the services you rendered before the Social Security Administration (SSA). List each meeting, conference, item of correspondence, telephone call, and other activity in which you engaged, such as research, preparation of a brief, attendance at a hearing, travel, etc., related to your services as representative in this case. Attach to this petition the list showing the dates, the descriptions of each service, the actual time spent in each, and the total hours.	
2.	Have you and your client entered into a fee agreement for services before SSA? If "yes," please specify the amount on which you agreed, and attach a copy of the agreement to this petition. $ _____	☐ YES ☐ NO and ☐ See attached
3.	(a) Have you received, or do you expect to receive, any payment toward your fee from any source other than from funds which SSA may be withholding for fee payment?	☐ YES ☐ NO
	(b) Do you currently hold in a trust or escrow account any amount of money you received toward payment of your fee?	☐ YES ☐ NO
	If "yes" to either or both of the above, please specify the source(s) and the amount(s). Source: _____ $ _____ Source: _____ $ _____ Note: If you receive payment(s) after submitting this petition, but before the SSA approves a fee, you have an affirmative duty to notify the SSA office to which you are sending this petition.	
4.	Have you received, or do you expect to receive, reimbursement for expenses you incurred? If "yes," please itemize your expenses and the amounts on a separate page.	☐ YES ☐ NO
5.	Did you render any services relating to this matter before any State or Federal court? If "yes," what fee did you or will you charge for services in connection with the court proceedings? $ _____ Please attach a copy of the court order if the court has approved a fee.	☐ YES ☐ NO

I certify that the information above, and on the attachment(s), is true and correct to the best of my knowledge and belief. I also certify that I have furnished a copy of this petition and the attachment(s) to the person(s) for whom I performed the services. I understand that failure to comply with Social Security laws and regulations pertaining to representation may result in suspension or disqualification from practice before SSA, the imposition of criminal penalties, or both.

Signature of Representative	Date	Address (include Zip Code)

Firm with which associated, if any	Telephone No. and Area Code

[Note: The following is optional. However, SSA can consider your fee petition more promptly if your client knows and already agrees with the amount you are requesting.]

I understand that I do not have to sign this petition or request. It is my right to disagree with the amount of the fee requested or any information given, and to ask more questions about the information given in this request (as explained on the reverse side of this form). I have marked my choice below.

☐ I agree with the $ _____ fee which my representative is asking to charge and collect. By signing this request, I am not giving up my right to disagree later with the total fee amount the Social Security Administration authorizes my representative to charge and collect.

OR

☐ I do not agree with the requested fee or other information given here, or I need more time. I understand that I must call, visit, or write to SSA within 20 days if I have questions or if I disagree with the fee requested or any information shown (as explained on the reverse sides of this form).

Signature of Claimant	Date

Address (include Zip Code)	Telephone No. and Area Code

Form SSA-1560-U4 (7-2000) EF (7-2000)
Destroy Prior Editions   FILE COPY

PETITION TO OBTAIN FEE APPROVAL

INSTRUCTIONS FOR USING THIS PETITION

Any attorney or other representative who wants to charge or collect a fee for services, rendered in connection with a claim before the Social Security Administration (SSA), is required by law to first obtain SSA's approval of the fee [sections 206(a) and 1631(d)(2) of the Social Security Act (42 U.S.C. 406(a) and 1383(d)(2)); section 413(b) of the Black Lung Benefits Act (30 U.S.C. 923(b)); and sections 404.1720, 410.686b, and 416.1520 of Social Security Administration Regulations Numbers 4, 10, and 16, respectively].

The only exceptions are if the fee is for services rendered (1) when a nonprofit organization or government agency pays the fee and any expenses out of funds which a government entity provided or administered and the claimant incurs no liability, directly or indirectly, for the cost of such services and expenses; (2) in an official capacity such as that of legal guardian, committee, or similar court-appointed office and the court has approved the fee in question; or (3) in representing the claimant before a court of law. A representative who has rendered services in a claim before both SSA and a court of law may seek a fee from either or both, but generally neither tribunal has the authority to set a fee for services rendered before the other [42 U.S.C. 406(a) and (b)].

When to File a Fee Petition

The representative should request fee approval only after completing all services (for the claimant and any auxiliaries). The representative has the option to petition either before or after SSA effectuates the determination(s).

In order to receive direct payment of all or any part of an authorized fee from past-due benefits, the attorney representative should file a request for fee approval, or written notice of intent to file a request, within 60 days of the date of the notice of the favorable determination is mailed. When there are multiple claims on one account and the attorney will not file the petition within 60 days after the mailing date of the first notice of favorable determination, he or she should file a written notice of intent to file a request for fee approval within the 60-day period.

Where to File the Petition

The representative must first give the "Claimant's Copy" of the SSA-1560-U4 petition to the claimant for whom he or she rendered services, with a copy of each attachment. The representative may then file the original and third carbon copy, the "OHA Copy," of the SSA-1560-U4, and the attachment(s), with the appropriate SSA office:

- If a court or the Appeals Council issued the decision, send the petition to the Office of Hearings and Appeals. Attention: Attorney Fee Branch, 5107 Leesburg Pike, Falls Church, VA 22041-3255.

- If an Administrative Law Judge issued the decision, send the petition to him or her using the hearing office address.

- In all other cases, send the petition to the reviewing office address which appears at the top right of the notice of award or notice of disapproved claim.

Evaluation of a Petition for a Fee

If the claimant has not agreed to and signed the fee petition, SSA does not begin evaluating the request for 30 days. SSA must decide what is a reasonable fee for the services rendered to the claimant, keeping in mind the purpose of the social security, black lung, or supplemental security income program. When evaluating a request for fee approval, SSA will consider the (1) extent and type of services the representative performed; (2) complexity of the case; (3) level of skill and competence required of the representative in giving the services; (4) amount of time he or she spent on the case; (5) results achieved; (6) levels of review to which the representative took the claim and at which he or she became the representative; and (7) amount of fee requested for services rendered, including any amount authorized or requested before but excluding any amount of expenses incurred.

SSA also considers the amount of benefits payable, if any, but authorizes the fee amount based on consideration of all the factors given here. The amount of benefits payable in a claim is determined by specific provisions of law unrelated to the representative's efforts. Also, the amount of past-due benefits may depend on the length of time that has elapsed since the claimant's effective date of entitlement.

Disagreement

SSA notifies both the representative and the claimant of the amount which it authorizes the representative to charge. If either or both disagree, SSA will further review the fee authorization when the claimant or representative sends a letter, explaining the reason(s) for disagreement, to the appropriate office within 30 days after the date of the notice of authorization to charge and receive a fee.

Collection of the Fee

Basic liability for payment of a representative's approved fee rests with the client. However, SSA will assist in fee collection when the representative is an attorney and SSA awards the claimant benefits under Title II of the Social Security Act or Title IV of the Federal Coal Mine Health and Safety Act of 1969, as amended. In these cases, SSA generally withholds 25 per cent of the claimant's past-due benefits. Once the fee is approved, SSA pays the attorney from the claimant's withheld funds. **This does not mean that SSA will approve as a reasonable fee 25 per cent of the past-due benefits.** The amount that is payable to the attorney from the withheld benefits is subject to the assessment required by section 206(d) of the Social Security Act, and it is also subject to offset by any fee payment(s) the attorney has received or expects to receive from an escrow or trust account. If the approved fee is more than the amount of the withheld benefits, collection of the difference is a matter between the attorney and the client.

Penalty for Charging or Collecting an Unauthorized Fee

Any individual who charges or collects an unauthorized fee for services provided in any claim, including services before a court which has rendered a favorable determination, may be subject to prosecution under 42 U.S.C. 406 and 1383 which provide that such individual, upon conviction thereof, shall for each offense be punished by a fine not exceeding $500, or by imprisonment not exceeding one year, or both. These penalties do not apply to fees for services performed before a court in supplemental security income claims because section 1383 provides no controls over such fees.

Computer Matching

We may also use the information you give us when we match records by computer. Matching programs compare our records with those of other Federal, State, or local government agencies. Many agencies may use matching programs to find or prove that a person qualifies for benefits paid by the Federal government. The law allows us to do this even if you do not agree to it.

Explanations about these and other reasons why information you provide us may be used or given out are available in Social Security Offices. If you want to learn more about this, contact any Social Security Office.

The Paperwork Reduction Act of 1995 requires us to notify you that this information collection is in accordance with the clearance requirements of section 3507 of the Paperwork Reduction Act of 1995. We may not conduct or sponsor, and you are not required to respond to, a collection of information unless it displays a valid OMB control number. We estimate that it will take you about 30 minutes to complete this form. This includes the time it will take to read the instructions, gather the necessary facts and fill out the form.

Form **SSA-1560-U4** (7-2000) EF (7-2000)
Destroy Prior Editions

SOCIAL SECURITY ADMINISTRATION

Form Approved
OMB No. 0960-0104

TOE 850

PETITION TO OBTAIN APPROVAL OF A FEE FOR REPRESENTING A CLAIMANT BEFORE THE SOCIAL SECURITY ADMINISTRATION

IMPORTANT
INFORMATION
ON REVERSE SIDE

PAPERWORK/PRIVACY ACT NOTICE: Your response to this request is voluntary, but the Social Security Administration may not approve any fee unless it receives the information this form requests. The Administration will use the information to determine a fair value for services you rendered to the claimant named below, as provided in section 206 of the Social Security Act (42 U.S.C. 406).

I request approval to charge a fee of ⟶ Fee $ _____ (Show the dollar amount)

for services performed as the representative of ⟶ Mr. ___ Mrs. ___ Ms. ___

My Services Began: ___ / ___ / ___
              Month Day   Year

Type(s) of claim(s) _____

My Services Ended: ___ / ___ / ___

Enter the name and the Social Security number of the person on whose Social Security record the claim is based _____
                                          ___ ___ ___ / ___ ___ / ___ ___ ___ ___

1.	Itemize on a separate page or pages the services you rendered before the Social Security Administration (SSA). List each meeting, conference, item of correspondence, telephone call, and other activity in which you engaged, such as research, preparation of a brief, attendance at a hearing, travel, etc., related to your services as representative in this case. Attach to this petition the list showing the dates, the descriptions of each service, the actual time spent in each, and the total hours.
2.	Have you and your client entered into a fee agreement for services before SSA? If "yes," please specify the amount on which you agreed, and attach a copy of the agreement to this petition. $ _____ ☐ YES ☐ NO and ☐ See attached
3.	(a) Have you received, or do you expect to receive, any payment toward your fee from any source other than from funds which SSA may be withholding for fee payment? ☐ YES ☐ NO (b) Do you currently hold in a trust or escrow account any amount of money you received toward payment of your fee? ☐ YES ☐ NO If "yes" to either or both of the above, please specify the source(s) and the amount(s). Source: _____ $ _____ Source: _____ $ _____ **Note:** If you receive payment(s) after submitting this petition, but before the SSA approves a fee, you have an affirmative duty to notify the SSA office to which you are sending this petition.
4.	Have you received, or do you expect to receive, reimbursement for expenses you incurred? If "yes," please itemize your expenses and the amounts on a separate page. ☐ YES ☐ NO
5.	Did you render any services relating to this matter before any State or Federal court? If "yes," what fee did you or will you charge for services in connection with the court proceedings? ☐ YES ☐ NO Please attach a copy of the court order if the court has approved a fee. $ _____

I certify that the information above, and on the attachment(s), is true and correct to the best of my knowledge and belief. I also certify that I have furnished a copy of this petition and the attachment(s) to the person(s) for whom I performed the services. I understand that failure to comply with Social Security laws and regulations pertaining to representation may result in suspension or disqualification from practice before SSA, the imposition of criminal penalties, or both.

Signature of Representative	Date	Address (include Zip Code)
Firm with which associated, if any		Telephone No. and Area Code

[Note: The following is optional. However, SSA can consider your fee petition more promptly if your client knows and already agrees with the amount you are requesting.]

I understand that I do not have to sign this petition or request. It is my right to disagree with the amount of the fee requested or any information given, and to ask more questions about the information given in this request (as explained on the reverse side of this form). I have marked my choice below.

☐   I agree with the $ _____ fee which my representative is asking to charge and collect. By signing this request, I am not giving up my right to disagree later with the total fee amount the Social Security Administration authorizes my representative to charge and collect.

                                     OR

☐   I do not agree with the requested fee or other information given here, or I need more time. I understand I must call, visit, or write to SSA within 20 days if I have questions or if I disagree with the fee requested or any information shown (as explained on the reverse sides of this form).

Signature of Claimant	Date
Address (include Zip Code)	Telephone No. and Area Code

Form SSA-1560-U4 (7-2000) EF (7-2000)
Destroy Prior Editions

CLAIMANT'S COPY

WHAT YOU SHOULD KNOW

This is a copy of a petition, or request, your representative made to the Social Security Administration (SSA) for approval to charge a fee for services performed in connection with your claim.

If You Have Questions or Disagree Now

If you have questions or if you disagree with the fee requested or any information shown, contact SSA **within 20 days** from the date of this request. You may call or visit your local Social Security office or you may write to the office which last took action in your case.

- Write to the SSA office address which appears at the top right on your notice of award or notice of disapproved claim, unless you know that your claim went to the Appeals Council or an Administrative Law Judge of the Office of Hearings and Appeals.

- If an Administrative Law Judge made the last decision in your case, write to him or her using the hearing office address.

- If the Appeals Council or a court made the last decision in your case, write to the Office of Hearings and Appeals, Attention: Attorney Fee Branch, 5107 Leesburg Pike, Falls Church, VA 22041-3255.

If you decide to call, visit, or write, act quickly so that your questions reach the correct office **within 20 days.**

For Your Protection

Until you receive notice that SSA has approved a fee, you should not pay your representative unless the payment is held in an escrow or trust account. If you are charged or pay any money after you receive your copy of this petition but before you receive notice of the fee amount your representative may charge, report this to SSA immediately.

What Happens Next

No matter what you may have agreed to in writing, SSA decides how much your representative may charge you for his or her services. SSA must decide what is a reasonable fee for the work your representative did, keeping in mind the purpose of the social security, black lung, or supplemental security income program. SSA **does not automatically approve 25 per cent of any past-due benefits as a reasonable fee.** SSA

must consider the (1) extent and type of services your representative performed; (2) complexity of your case; (3) level of skill and competence required of your representative in giving the services; (4) amount of time he or she spent on your case; (5) results achieved; (6) levels of review to which your representative took your claim and at which he or she became your representative; and (7) amount of fee he or she requests, including any amount requested or authorized before but excluding any amount of expenses incurred.

SSA also considers the amount of benefits payable, if any, but approves a fee amount based on all the factors given here. This is because the amount of benefits payable to you is determined by the law and regulations, not by your representative's efforts. Also, the amount of past-due benefits may depend on the length of time that has gone by since your effective date of entitlement.

What Happens Later

SSA will send you a written notice showing the fee amount your representative may charge you based on this request. If you disagree with the amount approved, you must write to say you disagree and to give your reasons, sending your letter to the SSA office address shown on the "Authorization to Charge and Receive a Fee" within 30 days of the date on that notice. **You may disagree with the fee approved, even if you do not disagree now with the fee amount your representative is requesting.**

The law and regulations say that part of any past-due social security or black lung benefits payable to you, under Title II of the Social Security Act or under Part B of Title IV of the Federal Coal Mine Health and Safety Act of 1969, as amended, must be used toward the payment of your representative's fee if he or she is an attorney at law. The amount SSA may pay your attorney directly is the smallest of the following:

- twenty-five per cent (25%), or one-fourth, of the total past-due benefits payable to you as a result of the

- the fee amount approved; or

- the amount which you and your attorney agreed upon as the fee for his or her services (shown on the reverse in item 2 of this petition).

The law does not permit SSA to pay representatives directly for services provided in connection with a claim for supplemental security income, under Title XVI of the Social Security Act.

Form **SSA-1560-U4** (7-2000) EF (7-2000)
Destroy Prior Editions

SOCIAL SECURITY ADMINISTRATION **TOE 850**

Form Approved
OMB No. 0960-0104

PETITION TO OBTAIN APPROVAL OF A FEE FOR REPRESENTING A CLAIMANT BEFORE THE SOCIAL SECURITY ADMINISTRATION

IMPORTANT
INFORMATION
ON REVERSE SIDE

PAPERWORK/PRIVACY ACT NOTICE: Your response to this request is voluntary, but the Social Security Administration may not approve any fee unless it receives the information this form requests. The Administration will use the information to determine a fair value for services you rendered to the claimant named below, as provided in section 206 of the Social Security Act (42 U.S.C. 406).

I request approval to charge a fee of ⟶ Fee $ _____ (Show the dollar amount)

for services performed as the representative of ⟶ Mr. Mrs. Ms. _____

My Services Began: ___ / ___ / ___
Month   Day   Year

Type(s) of claim(s) .

My Services Ended: ___ / ___ / ___

Enter the name and the Social Security number of the person on whose Social Security record the claim is based
___ ___ / ___ ___ / ___ ___ ___ ___

1. Itemize on a separate page or pages the services you rendered before the Social Security Administration (SSA). List each meeting, conference, item of correspondence, telephone call, and other activity in which you engaged, such as research, preparation of a brief, attendance at a hearing, travel, etc., related to your services as representative in this case. Attach to this petition the list showing the dates, the descriptions of each service, the actual time spent in each, and the total hours.

2. Have you and your client entered into a fee agreement for services before SSA? If "yes," please specify the amount on which you agreed, and attach a copy of the agreement to this petition. $ _____ □ YES □ NO and □ See attached

3. (a) Have you received, or do you expect to receive, any payment toward your fee from any source other than from funds which SSA may be withholding for fee payment? □ YES □ NO
(b) Do you currently hold in a trust or escrow account any amount of money you received toward payment of your fee? □ YES □ NO
If "yes" to either or both of the above, please specify the source(s) and the amount(s).
Source: _____ $ _____
Source: _____ $ _____
Note: If you receive payment(s) after submitting this petition, but before the SSA approves a fee, you have an affirmative duty to notify the SSA office to which you are sending this petition.

4. Have you received, or do you expect to receive, reimbursement for expenses you incurred? If "yes," please itemize your expenses and the amounts on a separate page. □ YES □ NO

5. Did you render any services relating to this matter before any State or Federal court? If "yes," what fee did you or will you charge for services in connection with the court proceedings? □ YES □ NO $ _____
Please attach a copy of the court order if the court has approved a fee.

I certify that the information above, and on the attachment(s), is true and correct to the best of my knowledge and belief. I also certify that I have furnished a copy of this petition and the attachment(s) to the person(s) for whom I performed the services. I understand that failure to comply with Social Security laws and regulations pertaining to representation may result in suspension or disqualification from practice before SSA, the imposition of criminal penalties, or both.

Signature of Representative   Date   Address (include Zip Code)

Firm with which associated, if any   Telephone No. and Area Code

[Note: The following is optional. However, SSA can consider your fee petition more promptly if your client knows and already agrees with the amount you are requesting.]

I understand that I do not have to sign this petition or request. It is my right to disagree with the amount of the fee requested or any information given, and to ask more questions about the information given in this request (as explained on the reverse side of this form). I have marked my choice below.

□ I agree with the $ _____ fee which my representative is asking to charge and collect. By signing this request, I am not giving up my right to disagree later with the total fee amount the Social Security Administration authorizes my representative to charge and collect.

OR

□ I do not agree with the requested fee or other information given here, or I need more time. I understand I must call, visit, or write to SSA within 20 days if I have questions or if I disagree with the fee requested or any information shown (as explained on the reverse sides of this form).

Signature of Claimant   Date

Address (include Zip Code)   Telephone No. and Area Code

Form **SSA-1560-U4** (7-2000) EF (7-2000)
Destroy Prior Editions

REPRESENTATIVE'S COPY

INSTRUCTIONS FOR USING THIS PETITION

Any attorney or other representative who wants to charge or collect a fee for services, rendered in connection with a claim before the Social Security Administration (SSA), is required by law to first obtain SSA's approval of the fee [sections 206(a) and 1631(d)(2) of the Social Security Act (42 U.S.C. 406(a) and 1383(d)(2)); section 413(b) of the Black Lung Benefits Act (30 U.S.C. 923(b)); and sections 404.1720, 410.686b, and 416.1520 of Social Security Administration Regulations Numbers 4, 10, and 16, respectively].

The only exceptions are if the fee is for services rendered (1) when a nonprofit organization or government agency pays the fee and any expenses out of funds which a government entity provided or administered and the claimant incurs no liability, directly or indirectly, for the cost of such services and expenses; (2) in an official capacity such as that of legal guardian, committee, or similar court-appointed office and the court has approved the fee in question; or (3) in representing the claimant before a court of law. A representative who has rendered services in a claim before both SSA and a court of law may settle a fee from either or both, but generally neither tribunal has the authority to set a fee for services rendered before the other [42 U.S.C. 406(a) and (b)].

When to File a Fee Petition

The representative should request fee approval only after completing all services (for the claimant and any auxiliaries). The representative has the option to petition either before or after SSA effectuates the determination(s).

In order to receive direct payment of all or any part of an authorized fee from past-due benefits, the attorney representative should file a request for fee approval, or written notice of intent to file a request, within 60 days of the date of the notice of the favorable determination is mailed. When there are multiple claims on one account and the attorney will not file the petition within 60 days after the mailing date of the first notice of favorable determination, he or she should file a written notice of intent to file a request for fee approval within the 60-day period.

Where to File the Petition

The representative must first give the "Claimant's Copy" of the SSA-1560-U4 petition to the claimant for whom he or she rendered services, with a copy of each attachment. The representative may then file the original and third carbon copy, the "OHA Copy," of the SSA-1560-U4, and the attachment(s), with the appropriate SSA office:

- If a court or the Appeals Council issued the decision, send the petition to the Office of Hearings and Appeals. Attention: Attorney Fee Branch, 5107 Leesburg Pike, Falls Church, VA 22041-3255.

- If an Administrative Law Judge issued the decision, send the petition to him or her using the hearing office address.

- In all other cases, send the petition to the reviewing office address which appears at the top right of the notice of award or notice of disapproved claim.

Evaluation of a Petition for a Fee

If the claimant has not agreed to and signed the fee petition, SSA does not begin evaluating the request for 30 days. SSA must decide what is a reasonable fee for the services rendered to the claimant, keeping in mind the purpose of the social security, black lung, or supplemental security income program. When evaluating a request for fee approval, SSA will consider the (1) extent and type of services the representative performed; (2) complexity of the case; (3) level of skill and competence required of the representative in giving the services; (4) amount of time he or she spent on the case; (5) results achieved; (6) levels of review to which the representative took the claim and at which he or she became the representative; and (7) amount of fee requested for services rendered, including any amount authorized or requested before but excluding any amount of expenses incurred.

SSA also considers the amount of benefits payable, if any, but authorizes the fee amount based on consideration of all the factors given here. The amount of benefits payable in a claim is determined by specific provisions of law unrelated to the representative's efforts. Also, the amount of past-due benefits may depend on the length of time that has elapsed since the claimant's effective date of entitlement.

Disagreement

SSA notifies both the representative and the claimant of the amount which it authorizes the representative to charge. If either or both disagree, SSA will further review the fee authorization when the claimant or representative sends a letter, explaining the reason(s) for disagreement, to the appropriate office within 30 days after the date of the notice of authorization to charge and receive a fee.

Collection of the Fee

Basic liability for payment of a representative's approved fee rests with the client. However, SSA will assist in fee collection when the representative is an attorney and SSA awards the claimant benefits under Title II of the Social Security Act or Title IV of the Federal Coal Mine Health and Safety Act of 1969, as amended. In these cases, SSA generally withholds 25 per cent of the claimant's past-due benefits. Once the fee is approved, SSA pays the attorney from the claimant's withheld funds. **This does not mean that SSA will approve as a reasonable fee 25 per cent of the past-due benefits.** The amount that is payable to the attorney from the withheld benefits is subject to the assessment required by section 206(d) of the Social Security Act, and it is also subject to offset by any fee payment(s) the attorney has received or expects to receive from an escrow or trust account. If the approved fee is more than the amount of the withheld benefits, collection of the difference is a matter between the attorney and the client.

Penalty for Charging or Collecting an Unauthorized Fee

Any individual who charges or collects an unauthorized fee for services provided in any claim, including services before a court which has rendered a favorable determination, may be subject to prosecution under 42 U.S.C. 406 and 1383 which provide that such individual, upon conviction thereof, shall for each offense be punished by a fine not exceeding $500, by imprisonment not exceeding one year, or both. These penalties do not apply to fees for services performed before a court in supplemental security income claims because section 1383 provides no controls over such fees.

Computer Matching

We may also use the information you give us when we match records by computer. Matching programs compare our records with those of other Federal, State, or local government agencies. Many agencies may use matching programs to find or prove that a person qualifies for benefits paid by the Federal government. The law allows us to do this even if you do not agree to it.

Explanations about these and other reasons why information you provide us may be used or given out are available in Social Security Offices. If you want to learn more about this, contact any Social Security Office.

The Paperwork Reduction Act of 1995 requires us to notify you that this information collection is in accordance with the clearance requirements of section 3507 of the Paperwork Reduction Act of 1995. We may not conduct or sponsor, and you are not required to respond to, a collection of information unless it displays a valid OMB control number. We estimate that it will take you about 30 minutes to complete this form. This includes the time it will take to read the instructions, gather the necessary facts and fill out the form.

Form **SSA-1560-U4** (7-2000) EF (7-2000)
Destroy Prior Editions

SOCIAL SECURITY ADMINISTRATION

TOE 850

Form Approved
OMB No. 0960-0104

PETITION TO OBTAIN APPROVAL OF A FEE FOR REPRESENTING A CLAIMANT BEFORE THE SOCIAL SECURITY ADMINISTRATION

IMPORTANT
INFORMATION
ON REVERSE SIDE

PAPERWORK/PRIVACY ACT NOTICE: Your response to this request is voluntary, but the Social Security Administration may not approve any fee unless it receives the information this form requests. The Administration will use the information to determine a fair value for services you rendered to the claimant named below, as provided in section 206 of the Social Security Act (42 U.S.C. 406).

I request approval to charge a fee of ⟶ | Fee $ | (Show the dollar amount)

for services performed as the representative of ⟶ | Mr. Mrs. Ms.

My Services Began: ___ / ___ / ___
         Month Day   Year

Type(s) of claim(s)

My Services Ended: ___ / ___ / ___

Enter the name and the Social Security number of the person on whose Social Security record the claim is based

___ ___ ___ / ___ ___ / ___ ___ ___ ___

1.	Itemize on a separate page or pages the services you rendered before the Social Security Administration (SSA). List each meeting, conference, item of correspondence, telephone call, and other activity in which you engaged, such as research, preparation of a brief, attendance at a hearing, travel, etc., related to your services as representative in this case. Attach to this petition the list showing the dates, the descriptions of each service, the actual time spent in each, and the total hours.	
2.	Have you and your client entered into a fee agreement for services before SSA? If "yes," please specify the amount on which you agreed, and attach a copy of the agreement to this petition. $_____ and	☐ YES ☐ NO ☐ See attached
3.	(a) Have you received, or do you expect to receive, any payment toward your fee from any source other than from funds which SSA may be withholding for fee payment?	☐ YES ☐ NO
	(b) Do you currently hold in a trust or escrow account any amount of money you received toward payment of your fee?	☐ YES ☐ NO
	If "yes" to either or both of the above, please specify the source(s) and the amount(s).	
	Source: _____ $ _____	
	Source: _____ $ _____	
	Note: If you receive payment(s) after submitting this petition, but before the SSA approves a fee, you have an affirmative duty to notify the SSA office to which you are sending this petition.	
4.	Have you received, or do you expect to receive, reimbursement for expenses you incurred? If "yes," please itemize your expenses and the amounts on a separate page.	☐ YES ☐ NO
5.	Did you render any services relating to this matter before any State or Federal court? If "yes," what fee did you or will you charge for services in connection with the court proceedings? $ _____	☐ YES ☐ NO
	Please attach a copy of the court order if the court has approved a fee.	

I certify that the information above, and on the attachment(s), is true and correct to the best of my knowledge and belief. I also certify that I have furnished a copy of this petition and the attachment(s) to the person(s) for whom I performed the services. I understand that failure to comply with Social Security laws and regulations pertaining to representation may result in suspension or disqualification from practice before SSA, the imposition of criminal penalties, or both.

Signature of Representative	Date	Address (include Zip Code)

Firm with which associated, if any	Telephone No. and Area Code

[Note: The following is optional. However, SSA can consider your fee petition more promptly if your client knows and already agrees with the amount you are requesting.]

I understand that I do not have to sign this petition or request. It is my right to disagree with the amount of the fee requested or any information given, and to ask more questions about the information given in this request (as explained on the reverse side of this form). I have marked my choice below.

☐   I agree with the $_____ fee which my representative is asking to charge and collect. By signing this request, I am not giving up my right to disagree later with the total fee amount the Social Security Administration authorizes my representative to charge and collect.

OR

☐   I do not agree with the requested fee or other information given here, or I need more time. I understand I must call, visit, or write to SSA within 20 days if I have questions or if I disagree with the fee requested or any information shown (as explained on the reverse sides of this form).

Signature of Claimant	Date

Address (include Zip Code)	Telephone No. and Area Code

Form SSA-1560-U4 (7-2000) EF (7-2000)
Destroy Prior Editions

OHA COPY

PETITION TO OBTAIN FEE APPROVAL

INSTRUCTIONS FOR USING THIS PETITION

Any attorney or other representative who wants to charge or collect a fee for services, rendered in connection with a claim before the Social Security Administration (SSA), is required by law to first obtain SSA's approval of the fee [sections 206(a) and 1631(d)(2) of the Social Security Act (42 U.S.C. 406(a) and 1383(d)(2)); section 413(b) of the Black Lung Benefits Act (30 U.S.C. 923(b)); and sections 404.1720, 410.686b, and 416.1520 of Social Security Administration Regulations Numbers 4, 10, and 16, respectively].

The only exceptions are if the fee is for services rendered (1) when a nonprofit organization or government agency pays the fee and any expenses out of funds which a government entity provided or administered and the claimant incurs no liability, directly or indirectly, for the cost of such services and expenses; (2) in an official capacity such as that of legal guardian, committee, or similar court-appointed office and the court has approved the fee in question; or (3) in representing the claimant before a court of law. A representative who has rendered services in a claim before both SSA and a court of law may seek a fee from either or both, but generally neither tribunal has the authority to set a fee for services rendered before the other [42 U.S.C. 406(a) and (b)].

When to File a Fee Petition

The representative should request fee approval only after completing all services (for the claimant and any auxiliaries). The representative has the option to petition either before or after SSA effectuates the determination(s).

In order to receive direct payment of all or any part of an authorized fee from past-due benefits, the attorney representative should file a request for fee approval, or written notice of intent to file a request, within 60 days of the date of the notice of the favorable determination is mailed. When there are multiple claims and the attorney will not file the petition within 60 days after the mailing date of the first notice of favorable determination, he or she should file a written notice of intent to file a request for fee approval within the 60-day period.

Where to File the Petition

The representative must first give the "Claimant's Copy" of the SSA-1560-U4 petition to the claimant for whom he or she rendered services, with a copy of each attachment. The representative may then file the original and third carbon copy, the "OHA Copy," of the SSA-1560-U4, and the attachment(s). with the appropriate SSA office:

- If a court or the Appeals Council issued the decision, send the petition to the Office of Hearings and Appeals. Attention: Attorney Fee Branch, 5107 Leesburg Pike, Falls Church, VA 22041-3255.

- If an Administrative Law Judge issued the decision, send the petition to him or her using the hearing office address.

- In all other cases, send the petition to the reviewing office address which appears at the top right of the notice of award or notice of disapproved claim.

Evaluation of a Petition for a Fee

If the claimant has not agreed to and signed the fee petition, SSA does not begin evaluating the request for 30 days. SSA must decide what is a reasonable fee for the services rendered to the claimant, keeping in mind the purpose of the social security, black lung, or supplemental security income program. When evaluating a request for fee approval, SSA will consider the (1) extent and type of services the representative performed; (2) complexity of the case; (3) level of skill and competence required of the representative in giving the services; (4) amount of time he or she spent on the case; (5) results achieved; (6) levels of review to which the representative took the claim and at which he or she became the representative; and (7) amount of fee requested for services rendered, including any amount authorized or requested before but excluding any amount of expenses incurred.

SSA also considers the amount of benefits payable, if any, but authorizes the fee amount based on consideration of all the factors given here. The amount of benefits payable in a claim is determined by specific provisions of law unrelated to the representative's efforts. Also, the amount of past-due benefits may depend on the length of time that has elapsed since the claimant's effective date of entitlement.

Disagreement

SSA notifies both the representative and the claimant of the amount which it authorizes the representative to charge. If either or both disagree, SSA will further review the fee authorization when the claimant or representative sends a letter, explaining the reason(s) for disagreement, to the appropriate office within 30 days after the date of the notice of authorization to charge and receive a fee.

Collection of the Fee

Basic liability for payment of a representative's approved fee rests with the client. However, SSA will assist in fee collection when the representative is an attorney and SSA awards the claimant benefits under Title II of the Social Security Act or Title IV of the Federal Coal Mine Health and Safety Act of 1969, as amended. In these cases, SSA generally withholds 25 per cent of the claimant's past-due benefits. Once the fee is approved, SSA pays the attorney from the claimant's withheld funds. **This does not mean that SSA will approve as a reasonable fee 25 per cent of the past-due benefits.** The amount that is payable to the attorney from the withheld benefits is subject to the assessment required by section 206(d) of the Social Security Act, and it is also subject to offset by any fee payment(s) the attorney has received or expects to receive from an escrow or trust account. If the approved fee is more than the amount of the withheld benefits, collection of the difference is a matter between the attorney and the client.

Penalty for Charging or Collecting an Unauthorized Fee

Any individual who charges or collects an unauthorized fee for services provided in any claim, including services before a court which has rendered a favorable determination, may be subject to prosecution under 42 U.S.C. 406 and 1383 which provide that such individual, upon conviction thereof, shall for each offense be punished by a fine not exceeding $500, by imprisonment not exceeding one year, or both. These penalties do not apply to fees for services performed before a court in supplemental security income claims because section 1383 provides no controls over such fees.

Computer Matching

We may also use the information you give us when we match records by computer. Matching programs compare our records with those of other Federal, State, or local government agencies. Many agencies may use matching programs to find or prove that a person qualifies for benefits paid by the Federal government. The law allows us to do this even if you do not agree to it.

Explanations about these and other reasons why information you provide us may be used or given out are available in Social Security Offices. If you want to learn more about this, contact any Social Security Office.

The Paperwork Reduction Act of 1995 requires us to notify you that this information collection is in accordance with the clearance requirements of section 3507 of the Paperwork Reduction Act of 1995. We may not conduct or sponsor, and you are not required to respond to, a collection of information unless it displays a valid OMB control number. We estimate that it will take you about 30 minutes to complete this form. This includes the time it will take to read the instructions, gather the necessary facts and fill out the form.

Form **SSA-1560-U4** (7-2000) EF (7-2000)
Destroy Prior Editions

Social Security Law

APPENDIX 24:
MODEL FEE AGREEMENT

FEE FOR SERVICES

My representative and I understand that, for a fee to be payable, the Social Security Administration (SSA) must approve any fee my representative charges or collects from me for services my representative provides in proceedings before the SSA in connection with my claim(s) for benefits.

We agree that, if the SSA favorably decides the claim(s), I will pay my representative a fee equal to the lesser of *[Insert a percent of past-due benefits (a number less than or equal to 25)]* or *[Insert a dollar amount (a number less than or equal to $5,300)]*.

REVIEW OF THE FEE

We understand that one or both of us may request review of the fee amount, in writing, within 15 days after the SSA has notified us of any amount my representative can charge.

My representative may ask the SSA to increase the fee, and *[Insert he or she]* has informed me that *[Insert he or she]* will do so if *[Insert the conditions under which the representative might seek a fee higher than the fee otherwise agreed upon]*.

I may ask the SSA to reduce the fee.

An affected auxiliary Social Security beneficiary, if any, may ask the SSA to reduce the fee too.

Also, if the SSA approved the fee agreement, the person(s) who decided my claim(s) may ask for a reduction of the fee under the agreement if, in his or her opinion, my representative did not represent my interests adequately or the fee is clearly excessive for the services provided.

If someone requests review, the SSA generally would send the other(s) a copy and offer an opportunity to comment on the request and provide more information to the person reviewing the request. The SSA then would finally decide the amount of the fee and notify us in writing whether the fee increased, decreased, or did not change.

We both have received signed copies of this agreement.

Date:

Claimant's Signature Line

Representative's Signature Line

GLOSSARY

Acknowledgement—A formal declaration of one's signature before a notary public.

Actuary—One who computes various insurance and property costs, and calculates the cost of life insurance risks and insurance premiums.

Administrator—The person appointed by the court to settle the estate of a deceased person if he or she dies intestate.

Affidavit—A sworn or affirmed statement made in writing and signed; if sworn, it is notarized.

American Bar Association (ABA)—A national organization of lawyers and law students.

American Civil Liberties Union (ACLU)—A nationwide organization dedicated to the enforcement and preservation of rights and civil liberties guaranteed by the federal and state constitutions.

Annuity—The right to receive fixed, periodic payments over a specified term.

Asset—The entirety of a person's property, either real or personal.

Assignee—An assignee is a person to whom an assignment is made, also known as a grantee.

Assignment—An assignment is the transfer of an interest in a right or property from one party to another.

Attending Physician—The doctor who is the primary caregiver for a particular patient.

Attestation—The act of witnessing an instrument in writing at the request of the party making the same, and subscribing it as a witness.

Attorney In Fact—An attorney-in-fact is an agent or representative of another given authority to act in that person's name and place pursuant to a document called a "power of attorney."

Beneficiary—As it pertains to Social Security benefits, a beneficiary is a person who receives Social Security and/or Supplemental Security Income (SSI) payments.

Bequest—Refers to a gift of personal property contained in a will.

Bill of Rights—The first eight amendments to the United States Constitution.

Capacity—Capacity is the legal qualification concerning the ability of one to understand the nature and effects of one's acts.

Chattel—Article of personal property.

Civil Rights Act of 1964—The federal act passed to provide stronger protection for rights guaranteed by the Constitution, such as voting rights.

Codicil—A document modifying an existing will which, in order to be valid, must be formally drafted and witnessed according to statutory requirements.

Collateral—Property which is pledged as additional security for a debt, such as a loan.

Community Property—A form of ownership in a minority of states where a husband and wife are deemed to own property in common, including earnings, each owning an undivided one-half interest in the property.

Consanguinity—Related by blood.

Conservator—A conservator is the court-appointed custodian of property belonging to a person determined to be unable to properly manage his or her property.

Consortium—The conjugal association of husband and wife, and the right of each to the company and care of the other.

Constitution—The fundamental principles of law which frame a governmental system.

Constitutional Right—Refers to the individual liberties granted by the constitution of a state or the federal government.

Coroner—The public official whose responsibility it is to investigate the circumstances and causes of deaths which occur within his or her jurisdiction.

Death Benefit—The amount of money paid to the surviving spouse of a deceased Social Security beneficiary under certain circumstances.

Decedent—A deceased person.

Decree—A decision or order of the court.

Deductible—An amount an insured person must pay before they are entitled to recover money from the insurer, in connection with a loss or expense covered by an insurance policy.

Deed—A legal instrument conveying title to real property.

Disability—Under the Social Security or Supplemental Security Income government programs, refers to the inability to do any substantial gainful activity because of a medically provable physical or mental impairment that is expected to result in death, or that has lasted, or is expected to last, at least 12 continuous months.

Domicile—The one place designated as an individual's permanent home.

Due Process Rights—All rights which are of such fundamental importance as to require compliance with due process standards of fairness and justice.

Durable Power of Attorney—Also known as a "health care proxy," refers to a document naming a person to make a medical decisions in the event that the individual becomes unable to make those decisions himself or herself.

Duress—Refers to the action of one person which compels another to do something he or she would not otherwise do.

Duty—The obligation, to which the law will give recognition and effect, to conform to a particular standard of conduct toward another.

Earned Income—Income which is gained through one's labor and services, as opposed to investment income.

Elective Share—Statutory provision that a surviving spouse may choose between taking that which is provided in the spouse's will, or taking a statutorily prescribed share.

Employee Retirement Income Security Act of 1974 (ERISA)—A federal statute which governs the administration of pension plans.

Equitable Distribution—The power of the courts to equitably distribute all property legally and beneficially acquired during marriage by either spouse, whether legal title lies in their joint or individual names.

Estate—The entirety of one's property, real or personal.

Estate Tax—A tax levied on a decedent's estate in connection with the right to transfer property after death.

Execution—The performance of all acts necessary to render a written instrument complete, such as signing, sealing, acknowledging, and delivering the instrument; also refers to supplementary proceedings to enforce a judgment, which, if monetary, involves a direction to the sheriff to take the necessary steps to collect the judgment.

Executor—A person appointed by the maker of a will to carry out his or her wishes concerning the administration and distribution of his or estate according to the terms of a will.

Executor's Deed—A deed given by an executor or other fiduciary which conveys real property.

Exemption—A tax deduction granted a taxpayer who has a certain status, e.g. aged 65 or over.

Face Value—The value of an insurance policy upon the death of the insured.

Fiduciary—A fiduciary is a person having a legal duty, created by an undertaking, to act primarily for the benefit of another in matters connected with the undertaking.

Fixed Income—Income which is unchangeable.

Fraud—A false representation of a matter of fact, whether by words or by conduct, by false or misleading allegations, or by concealment of that which should have been disclosed, which deceives and is intended to deceive another, and thereby causes injury to that person.

Fraudulent Conveyance—The transfer of property for the purpose of delaying or defrauding creditors.

Guardian—A person who is entrusted with the management of the property and/or person of another who is incapable, due to age or incapacity, to administer their own affairs.

Guardian Ad Litem—Person appointed by a court to represent a minor or incompetent for purpose of some litigation.

Heir—One who inherits property.

Heirs—Those individuals who, by law, inherit an estate of an ancestor who dies without a will.

Hereditament—Anything which can be inherited.

Hereditary Succession—The passing of title to an estate according to the laws of descent.

Illegal—Against the law.

Incapacity—Incapacity is a defense to breach of contract which refers to a lack of legal, physical or intellectual power to enter into a contract.

Incompetency—Lack of legal qualification or fitness to discharge a legally required duty or to handle one's own affairs; also refers to matters not admissible in evidence.

Indigent—A person who is financially destitute.

Individual Retirement Account (IRA)—A retirement plan for individuals who are not eligible for pension or profit-sharing plans.

Inherit—To take as an heir at law by descent rather than by will.

Inheritance—Property inherited by heirs according to the laws of descent and distribution.

Inheritance Tax—A tax levied on heirs in connection with the right to receive property from a decedent's estate.

Insurance—A contingency agreement, supported by consideration, whereby the insured receives a benefit, e.g. money, in the event the contingency occurs.

Intestate—The state of dying without having executed a valid will.

Intestate Succession—The manner of disposing of property according to the laws of descent and distribution when the decedent died without leaving a valid will.

Joint Tenancy—The ownership of property by two or more persons who each have an undivided interest in the whole property, with the right of survivorship, whereby upon the death of one joint tenant, the remaining joint tenants assume ownership.

Legacy—A gift of personal property by will.

Legal Aid—A national organization established to provide legal services to those who are unable to afford private representation.

Legal Capacity—Referring to the legal capacity to sue, it is the requirement that a person bringing the lawsuit have a sound mind, be of lawful age, and be under no restraint or legal disability.

Legatee—One who takes a legacy.

Letters of Administration—A formal document issued by a court which authorizes a person to act as an administrator for the estate of a deceased person.

Life Expectancy—The period of time which a person is statistically expected to live, based on such factors as their present age and sex.

Life Insurance—A contract between an insured and an insurer whereby the insurer promises to pay a sum of money upon the death of the insured to his or her designated beneficiary, in return for the periodic payment of money, known as a premium.

Living Trust—A trust which is operated during the life of the creator of the trust.

Living Will—A declaration that states an individual's wishes concerning the use of extraordinary life support systems.

Long-Term Care—The services provided at home or in an institutionalized setting to older persons who require medical or personal care for an extended period of time.

Marital Property—Property purchased by persons while married to each other.

Medicare—The program governed by the Social Security Administration to provide medical and hospital coverage to the aged or disabled.

Minor—A person who has not yet reached the age of legal competence, which is designated as 18 in most states.

Net Estate—The gross estate less the decedent's debts, funeral expenses and any other deductions proscribed by law.

Net Income—Gross income less deductions and exemptions proscribed by law.

Net Worth—The difference between one's assets and liabilities.

Oath—A sworn declaration of the truth under penalty of perjury.

Ombudsman—Under certain state laws, an individual licensed to oversee various health care issues.

Parens Patriae—Latin for "parent of his country." Refers to the role of the state as guardian of legally disabled individuals.

Party—Person having a direct interest in a legal matter, transaction or proceeding.

Pension Benefits—An amount of money paid to an employee upon retirement based upon such factors as salary and length of employment.

Pension Plan—A retirement plan established by an employer for the payment of pension benefits to employees upon retirement.

Petition—A formal written request to a court which initiates a special proceeding.

Petitioner—In a special proceeding, one who commences a formal written application, requesting some action or relief, addressed to a court for determination.

Power of Attorney—A legal process where one individual grants a third party the authority to transact certain business for that individual. It does not diminish the rights of the individual and does not usually grant the third party the right to manage the individual's assets.

Premium—The periodic payment of money by an insured to an insurer for insurance protection against specified losses.

Probate—The process of proving the validity of a will and administering the estate of a decedent.

Representativer Payee—A representative payee is an individual or organization that receives Social Security and/or SSI payments for someone who cannot manage or direct the management of his/her money.

Residuary Clause—The clause in a will which conveys to the residuary beneficiaries any property of the testator which was not specifically given to a particular legatee.

Statute—A law.

Succession—The process by which a decedent's property is distributed, either by will or by the laws of descent and distribution.

Successor—One who takes the place of another and continues in their position.

Supplemental Security Income (SSI)—The government program awarding cash benefits to the needy, aged, blind or otherwise qualifying disabled.

Surety—A surety is one who undertakes to pay money or perform in the event that the principal fails to do so.

Surrogate—A person appointed to act in place of another.

Taxable Estate—The decedent's gross estate less applicable statutory estate tax deductions, such as charitable deductions.

Tenancy by the Entirety—A form of ownership available only to a husband and wife whereby they each are deemed to hold title to the whole property, with right of survivorship.

Tenancy in Common—An ownership of real estate by two or more persons, each of whom has an undivided fractional interest in the whole property, without any right of survivorship.

Terminal Illness—An incurable condition caused by injury, disease or illness which, regardless of the application of life-sustaining procedures would, within reasonable medical judgment, produce death and where the application of life-sustaining procedures serve only to postpone the moment of death of the patient.

Testate—The state of dying with a valid will in place.

Testator—A male individual who makes and executes a will.

Testatrix—A female individual who makes and executes a will.

Testify—The offering of a statement in a judicial proceeding, under oath and subject to the penalty of perjury.

Testimony—The sworn statement make by a witness in a judicial proceeding.

Trust—The transfer of property, real or personal, to the care of a trustee, with the intention that the trustee manage the property on behalf of another person.

Unconscionable—Refers to a bargain so one-sided as to amount to an absence of meaningful choice on the part of one of the parties, together with terms which are unreasonably favorable to the other party.

Unconstitutional—Refers to a statute which conflicts with the United States Constitution rendering it void.

Underwrite—In insurance law, it refers to the assumption of the risk of loss to the insured's person or property, by the insurer of the insurance policy.

Uniform Laws—Laws that have been approved by the Commissioners on Uniform State Laws, and which are proposed to all state legislatures for consideration and adoption.

Vested—The right to receive, either at present or in the future, a certain benefit, such as a pension from an employer, without further conditions, such as continued employment.

Waiver—An intentional and voluntary surrender of a right.

Ward—A person over whom a guardian is appointed to manage his or her affairs.

Will—A legal document which a person executes setting forth their wishes as to the distribution of their property upon death.

Witness—One who testifies to what he has seen, heard, or otherwise observed.

X—Refers to the mark that may be used to denote one's signature when the signer is unable to write his or her name.

BIBLIOGRAPHY AND SUGGESTED READING

The Administration on Aging (Date Visited: April 2004) <http://www.aoa.gov/>.

American Association of Retired Persons (AARP) (Date Visited: April 2004) <http://www.aarp.org/>.

American Bar Association Commission on Legal Problems of the Elderly (Date Visited: April 2004) <http://www.abanet.org/>.

Black's Law Dictionary, Fifth Edition. St. Paul, MN: West Publishing Company, 1979.

Center for Medicare Advocacy (Date Visited: April 2004) <http://www.medicareadvocacy.org/>.

The Centers for Medicare & Medicaid Services (Date Visited: April 2004) <http://www.medicare.gov/>.

The Hospice Patient's Alliance (Date Visited: April 2004) <http://www.hospicepatients.org/>.

Internal Revenue Service (Date Visited: April 2004) <http://www.irs.ustreas.gov/>.

The Medicare Rights Center (Date Visited: April 2004) <http://www.medicarerights.org/>.

National Academy of Elder Law Attorneys (Date Visited: April 2004) <http://www.naela.org/>.

National Center for Health Statistics (Date Visited: April 2004)<http://www.cdc.gov/nchswww/howto/w2w/w2welcom.htm/>.

The National Institute on Aging (Date Visited: April 2004) <http://www.nia.nih.gov/>.

National Senior Citizens Law Center (Date Visited: April 2004) <http://www.nsclc.org/>.

The Social Security Administration (Date Visited: April 2004) <http://www.socialsecurity.gov/>.

The United States Census Bureau (Date Visited: April 2004) <http://www.census.gov/>.

Monthly Vital Statistics Report, Life Expectancy Tables. U.S. Department of Health (Date Visited: April 2004) <http://www.cdc.gov/nchs/>.

United States Department of Health and Human Services Office of Disability, Aging and Long-Term Care (Date Visited: April 2004) <http://aspe.os.dhhs.gov/daltcp/home>.

United States Department of Labor, Pension and Welfare Benefits Administration (Date Visited: April 2004) <http://www.dol.gov/dol/pwba>.